Managing Generation Z

Generation Z (Gen Z) is the young generation born between the mid-1990s and 2010s. They are now entering the market and starting their first jobs. Therefore, managers must shape the company workplace environment to encourage young employees to work efficiently and connect their future with the company. Only then will both managers and employees share mutual satisfaction from collaboration and aim at the common target, which should be the prosperity of the company. This book presents research results and techniques for analysing the working expectations and needs of Gen Z. The analyses were made in various countries in Europe: The Czech Republic, Latvia, Poland, and Portugal.

The book contains chapters that present the analysis results and technical chapters that outline modern methods of analysis of management data, including tutorial chapters on machine learning, which currently makes a strong appearance in research in various disciplines. This volume will be of interest to researchers, academics, practitioners, and students in the fields of management studies, research methods, and human resource management.

Joanna Nieżurawska is Doctor of Economics in the discipline of Management Sciences, Trainer in the field of Human Resource Management, and Contractor at Wyzsza Szkola Bankowa University, Toruń, Poland.

Radosław Antoni Kycia is Researcher in the Department of Mathematics and Statistics at Masaryk University, Brno, Czechia and Assistant Professor at the Faculty of Computer Science and Telecommunications of Tadeusz Kościuszko Cracow University of Technology, Kraków, Poland.

Agnieszka Niemczynowicz is Research Associate in the Department of Analysis and Differential Equations at University of Warmia and Mazury, Olsztyn, Poland.

Routledge Open Business and Economics

Routledge Open Business and Economics provides a platform for the open access publication of monographs and edited collections across the full breadth of these disciplines including accounting, finance, management, marketing and political economy. Reflecting our commitment to supporting open access publishing, this series provides a key repository for academic research in business and economics.

Books in the series are published via the Gold Open Access model and are therefore available for free download and re-use according to the terms of Creative Commons licence. They can be accessed via the Routledge and Taylor & Francis website, as well as third party discovery sites such as the Directory of OAPEN Library, Open Access Books, PMC Bookshelf, and Google Books.

Note that the other Business and Economics series at Routledge also all accept open access books for publication.

Managing Generation Z
Motivation, Engagement and Loyalty
Edited by Joanna Nieżurawska, Radosław Antoni Kycia and Agnieszka Niemczynowicz

Higher Education Institutions and Digital Transformation
Building University-Enterprise Collaborative Relationships
Marcin Lis

For more information about this series, please visit: www.routledge.com/ Routledge-Open-Business-and-Economics/book-series/ROBE

Managing Generation Z

Motivation, Engagement
and Loyalty

**Edited by Joanna Nieżurawska,
Radosław Antoni Kycia and Agnieszka
Niemczynowicz**

Routledge
Taylor & Francis Group

NEW YORK AND LONDON

First published 2023
by Routledge
605 Third Avenue, New York, NY 10158

and by Routledge
4 Park Square, Milton Park, Abingdon, Oxon, OX14 4RN

Routledge is an imprint of the Taylor & Francis Group, an informa business

Library of Congress Cataloging-in-Publication Data
Names: Nieżurawska, Joanna, editor. | Kycia, Radosław Antoni, editor. |
    Niemczynowicz, Agnieszka, editor.
Title: Managing Generation Z : motivation, engagement and loyalty /
    edited by Joanna Nieżurawska-Zając, Radosław Antoni Kycia and
    Agnieszka Niemczynowicz.
Description: New York, NY : Routledge, 2023. | Series: Routledge open
    business and economics | Includes bibliographical references and index.
Identifiers: LCCN 2022052731 | ISBN 9781032406084 (hardback) |
    ISBN 9781032406091 (paperback) | ISBN 9781003353935 (ebook)
Subjects: LCSH: Personnel management—Europe. | Generation Z—Europe.
Classification: LCC HF5549.2.E85 M36 2023 | DDC 658.30094—dc23/
    eng/20230110
LC record available at https://lccn.loc.gov/2022052731

ISBN: 978-1-032-40608-4 (hbk)
ISBN: 978-1-032-40609-1 (pbk)
ISBN: 978-1-003-35393-5 (ebk)

DOI: 10.4324/9781003353935

Typeset in Times New Roman
by Apex CoVantage, LLC

To my kids—Viki, Kacper, and Olivier, Joanna Nieżurawska

To my family,
Radosław Antoni Kycia

To my daughters—Julia and Aleksandra,
Agnieszka Niemczynowicz

Contents

Figures

Tables

List of authors

Nelson Duarte is a PhD in Management, Coordinating Professor at the School of Management and Technology of Porto Polytechnic, Researcher at INESC TEC and at International Research Institute for Economics and Management, and Director at the International Engineering and Technology Institute. The main areas of intervention are business models, strategy, entrepreneurship and innovation, project management, sustainability, and digital transformation.

Radosław Antoni Kycia is a researcher in the Department of Mathematics and Statistics at Masaryk University, Brno, Czechia and an assistant professor at the Faculty of Computer Science and Telecommunications of Tadeusz Kościuszko Cracow University of Technology, Krakow, Poland.

Iveta Ludviga is a full professor and Postgraduate Study Programme Director of RISEBA University of Applied Sciences, Latvia.

Agnieszka Niemczynowicz is a research associate in the Department of Analysis and Differential Equations at University of Warmia and Mazury, Olsztyn, Poland.

Joanna Nieżurawska is a doctor of economics in the discipline of management sciences, a trainer in the field of human resource management, a research associate in the Department of Finance and Management at Wyzsza Szkola Bankowa University, Torun, Poland, and President of MIERO Foundation.

Carla Pereira is a PhD in informatics engineering, Coordinating Professor at the School of Management and Technology of Porto Polytechnic, and Senior Researcher at INESC TEC. The main areas of intervention are business innovation, entrepreneurship and technology transfer, collaborative networks, information and knowledge management, and digital transformation.

Inese Sluka is a PhD student and Programme Director of RISEBA University of Applied Sciences, Latvia.

Acknowledgements

Radosław Kycia wants to thank his family for continuous support at every stage of his life. He also wishes to thank his collaborators: Agnieszka Niemczynowicz and Joanna Nieżurawska, for the perfect collaboration on this book and the Gen Z Project.

Agnieszka Niemczynowicz would like to acknowledge the team of the Gen Z Project for fruitful cooperation, especially Joanna Nieżurawska for initiating the research on Gen Z and for the excellent coordination of the Gen Z Project. Special thanks to Radosław Kycia for much helpful research discussions and support during the realization of the Gen Z Project. The last thanks goes to her daughters—Julia and Aleksandra—for their patience and dedicated support of their mother's work.

They want to thank Brianna Ascher and Alexandra Atkinson from Routledge for their assistance during the publication process.

This material has been supported by the Polish National Agency for Academic Exchange under Grant No. PPI/APM/2019/1/00017/U/00001.

1 Preface

Joanna Nieżurawska, Radosław Antoni Kycia, and Agnieszka Niemczynowicz

Generation Z (Gen Z) is the young generation born between the mid-1990s and 2010s. Currently, they enter the market, starting their first jobs. Therefore, managers need to shape the company workplace environment to encourage young employees to work efficiently and for them to connect their future with the company. Only then will both managers and employees share mutual satisfaction from collaboration and aim at the common target, which should be the prosperity of the company.

The book you are holding presents research results and techniques for analysing working expectations and needs of Gen Z. The analyses were made in various countries of Europe: The Czech Republic, Latvia, Poland, Portugal.

The book describes the analysis of motivation of Gen Z from Europe since we are Europe-based. However, the methods described in the book can be easily applied, without alteration, to the North America region. Therefore, the material in the book can be treated as a case study or an example of how to organise such research. The methods are fairly general and can be adjusted to other similar studies.

This book will be useful for:

- Scientists that specialise in motivation systems and analyse various sociological data that include Gen Z.
- Students that want to understand trends in current management and sociological research and to pick up some modern research methods in management and sociology.
- Managers and hobbyists that are interested in the motivation of Gen Z, their motivation, and general scheme of management research.

The book contains chapters that present results of the analysis and technical chapters that outline modern methods of analysis of management data, including tutorial chapters on machine learning, which currently makes a strong appearance in research in various disciplines.

DOI: 10.4324/9781003353935-1

The scientific methods, presented on the example of Gen Z, can be applied literally to other demographic cohorts since the methods are general enough to be easily adjusted.

We would be glad to know your opinion or remarks about the material in this book. Please contact us at: j.niezurawska@interia.pl

Joanna Nieżurawska	Toruń
Radosław Antoni Kycia	Brno, Kraków
Agnieszka Niemczynowicz	Olsztyn
	2022

1.1 How to read the book

The book is divided into seven chapters, including this Preface. You can cherry-pick the chapters you are the most interested in and dive into the details. We provide some suggestions on how to do it effectively. If you are:

- *A beginner to the subject of motivating Generation Z* (e.g., a student or researcher in other fields), then the optimal choice will be to start from the Introduction and then continue with Chapter 3. For an example of more quantitative studies, you should read also Chapter 4. If you are interested in how to make questionnaires for such research, then the Appendices will also be interesting for you.
- *An entrepreneur*, then you should read Chapter 7 where the specific advices are provided for practitioners.
- *Interested in modern computer science methods to analyse management data*, including motivating of Gen Z, then you should start with Chapter 5 where the general overview of programming in Python language is provided along with a lot of practical advices. It is a hands-on approach, so you should be ready to experiment with the code as you read. Then you should read Chapter 6, where some examples of machine learning methods were provided with ready-to-use recipes in management research.
- *A researcher active in the field of motivating Gen Z*, you will probably be interested in skimming the Introduction and then reading Chapters 3, 4, and 7. Moreover, if you want to employ modern computer methods in your research, then Chapters 5 and 6 will be of importance to you. You can also check the Appendices for example questionnaires ready to employ in your research.

We wish you a lot of new ideas during the lecture of our book!

2 Introduction

*Joanna Nieżurawska, Radosław Antoni Kycia,
and Agnieszka Niemczynowicz*

The changes taking place in the economy, in particular the development of
the knowledge-based economy, forced employers to change their approach
to motivating employees. The reason for this is the growing awareness that
people are the company's most valuable resource, in which companies
should constantly invest. Investing in employees manifests itself not only
by subsidising their education but also by investing in their health, including tools supporting work-life balance, as well as environmental protection
and activities related to responsible business. In enterprises, investing in
employees is correlated with the implementation of appropriate instruments
and concepts of motivating and building a coherent, integrated policy of
motivating employees.

Even though both in theory and practice, many systemic solutions have
been developed for motivating employees, and companies are outdoing
each other in implementing newer instruments and concepts of motivating, research in recent years indicates a significant decrease in the level
of commitment and loyalty of employees in the European Union, including a decline in the level of engagement [1]. The phenomenon causes
perturbations in enterprises, generates an increase in costs, causes poorer
work results, and a greater turnover of staff. To prevent this, employers are
looking for new solutions in the area of human resource management. It is
becoming imperative to introduce modern motivational concepts so as to
increase the level of commitment and loyalty among employees. It becomes
all the more difficult as the priorities and expectations towards work change
as the standard of living increases. They remain diversified in the cross
section of a huge number of factors differentiating labour resources, among
which age plays a huge role.

In the first decade of the 21st century, motivation takes on a new dimension. It turns out that currently the problem is not just attracting the right
employees to the organisation but most of all their retention and working
with a high level of engagement [2]. Therefore, the biggest problem for

DOI: 10.4324/9781003353935-2

enterprises is to maintain a high level of employee engagement and loyalty. New solutions in this area should go a step further and serve to shape the professional activity of employees, with particular emphasis on the stability of employee attitudes that influence commitment and loyalty. Taking into account the diversification of employee groups, the concepts should constitute the foundation based on which the instruments of motivating measures are created, aimed at satisfying different needs, expectations, and aspirations of employees, aimed at building a sense of happiness at work, maintaining a balance between work and life, as well as material status.

In this context, the issue of effective motivation of employees representing different generations is an important scientific problem. The issue has been only partially indicated in the literature on the subject and mostly refers to the identification of employees' needs and expectations as part of the undertaken motivational activities. There is a gap in this respect, which has become a premise for undertaking the research presented in this monograph.

In Europe and the world, modern motivational concepts have been developed in many ways. However, there is still no comprehensive research on their impact on the level of employee engagement and loyalty. Moreover, there is a noticeable shortage of comprehensive research on the usefulness of modern motivational concepts in the understanding of the sources of motivation to work and, consequently, motivating employees of different generations. The European and world literature presents the results of analyses of system solutions in the field of modern motivational concepts, while generational diversity and its influence on the selection of appropriate motivating concepts are only a fragment of this research.

An important problem discussed in this study is the change in the labour market, which led to the emergence of a new phenomenon—generation diversity. Currently, there are four generations of employees on the labour market: BB, X, Y, and Z. The problem is not the presence of many groups— there have always been employees of various ages in the labour market— what is crucial is how vast the differences between the generations are. The differences can be seen, for example, in approach to work, in attitudes and relations between the oldest and the youngest generations. Certain generational groups have already been studied in the literature on the subject; millennials (Generation Y) are most accurately described. However, comprehensive studies comparing the four generations are lacking. Analyses showing the effectiveness of the implementation of the motivation concept contain a clear gap, because they do not diagnose the impact of these concepts on building engagement and loyalty of employees of the BB, X, Y, and Z generation. This is due to the lack of a comprehensive diagnosis of the youngest generation Z and their preferences in terms of motivation. In the future, Generation Z in particular will be the object of analysis by researchers and employers. Employers' uncertainty is also raised by the oldest generation—the BB generation. Many changes in the economic environment affect employers' decisions about employing older people. In surveyed countries, this process results from the observed demographic changes, the aging of the population in particular.

Taking up the issues of modern concepts of motivating, which accounts for generational diversity, comes mainly from cognitive motives but also has practical justification. A possibly comprehensive presentation of not only traditional solutions in the field of motivation, but especially of the modern concepts such as the concept of work-life balance, cafeteria systems, and hygge may influence the creation of system solutions in the field of motivation. Systems which will effectively use these concepts in age management.

The following research questions have been formulated:

1. Why is Gen Z so different from the other ones?
2. How to motivate Gen Z employees?
3. How to increase engagement and loyalty of Gen Z at the workplace?
4. How to employ modern data analysis and machine learning into management research?

Many research methods were required to answer the research questions. The theoretical part of the work was created as a result of literary studies. In the empirical part, quantitative research methods were used: questionnaire research, selected statistical methods including correlations, dimensionality reduction in terms of principal component analysis, clustering methods as k-means, and econometric modelling.

The book is a result of multinational collaboration including researchers from Masaryk University (the Czech Republic), University of Warmia and Mazury in Olsztyn (Poland), WSB University in Toruń (Poland), RISEBA University (Latvia) and Porto Polytechnic (Portugal). The blend of different experiences of researchers from many countries in Europe results in its hard mimic style.

An original questionnaire was used to conduct the research, which was sent to Generation Z in Poland, Portugal, and Latvia.

The *SPSS programme* and the Smart-PLS software were used to develop the empirical material. For research purposes, the loyalty index and *the employee engagement index* have been distinguished, which made it possible to diagnose the effectiveness of the incentive policy.

In order to draw conclusions from the relationship between non-measurable concepts, based on non-experimental data, *the method of structural equations modelling*[1] was used [3]. The structural equation modelling

(PLS-SEM) technique based on variance was used to test the model and to forecast the most important factors relevant to employee engagement and loyalty. The book also presents machine learning methods.

The multiplicity and variety of methods used in the study allowed to obtain a wide range of information on motivating employees in groups of different generations and factors increasing employee engagement and loyalty, as well as to select research methods that seem most appropriate in the area of motivation.

Note

1 Blunch N.J. (2013), *Introduction to Structural Equation Modelling using IBM SPSS Statistics and AMOS*, 2nd edition, International Ed.: SAGE.

Bibliography

[1] Trends in Global Employee Engagement (2017), Source. www.aon.com/engagement17/index.aspx (accessed: 10.01.2019).
[2] Gruman J.A., Saks A.M. (2011), *Performance management and employee engagement*, Human Resource Management Review, 21(2), 123–136. Guest D.E. (2013), *Employee engagement: Fashionable fad or long-term fixture?*, in *Employee Engagement in Theory and Practice*, ed. Truss C., Deldridge R., Alfes K., Shants A., Soane E., London: Routledge, p. 231.
[3] Blunch, N.J. (2013), *Introduction to Structural Equation Modelling using IBM SPSS Statistics and AMOS*, 2nd edition, International Ed.: SAGE.

3 Motivation of Generation Z

Joanna Nieżurawska

3.1 Motivation and motivating Generation Z

Motivating is shaping motivation in a desired and acceptable way. Motivation is inextricably linked with concepts such as *motive and stimulus.* A motive stimulates the organism to behave in a given way and provides a person with a reason to behave in a certain way. In the process of motivation, stimuli engage a person to achieve specific goals, i.e. they are responsible for evoking motives. *The stimulus is an element of the situation* in which the subject is found, so it is always outside the individual. *The motive, on the other hand, is the mental state* of the subject and is always internal. Motivation is not only the engine of human behaviour but is also a factor in increasing work efficiency. Many studies also show a relationship between proper motivation and increased commitment. The employee's motivation is permanently shaped by the implementation of appropriate incentive instruments, and these instruments should be implemented systemically and comprehensively [28].

The outlining of realistic objectives for the company and engaging the personnel supports the motivation system of a company. The design of motivational programmes is aimed at optimal use of the available human resources in order to achieve the company's objectives, while allowing for better familiarisation and development of the employee's personality. Motivation systems are composed so as to generate conditions that are beneficial for the motivation of all employees in the company. They are to affect personnel psychologically as well as economically (both aspects are of equal significance). Motivation systems are also utilised in the scope of the adaptation program. In such case, it is in the form of a set of facts in document form. It influences and motivates employees according to the company's production and trade objectives or its business plans [9].

During the first ten years of the 21st century, motivation took on a completely new dimension. Nowadays attracting the right employees to the

DOI: 10.4324/9781003353935-3

company is not the only difficulty, keeping them and motivating them to work with a high level of engagement also became an issue. As a result maintaining a high degree of employee engagement and loyalty by introduction of accordingly designed motivation programmes is the largest problem for companies. Previously solutions in scope of motivation were focused on flexibility and individualism. Numerous outstanding scientific papers were written, and research was conducted on this subject in many different countries [3], [7]. New solutions in this area should venture further and assist in shaping the professional activity of employees, with particular emphasis placed on the sustainability of employee attitudes that influence engagement and loyalty. Considering the diversification of employee groups, the concepts should constitute the foundation for the creation of the tools of motivation. Their objective should be to satisfy the varying needs, expectations, and aspirations of employees, to build a sense of happiness at work, maintain a balance between work and private life, as well as material status.

In the above context, the matter of effective motivating of employees coming from various generations is a significant scientific problem, and in particular when it comes to Generation Z. In literature on the subject this issue has only been partially considered, and mostly in reference to the identification of employees' needs and expectations in the scope of motivational activities [3, 15, 25]. The research presented in this article was undertaken in order to fill the gap that exists in this respect.

3.1.1 Motivation theories

Motivation theories are described in great detail in the literature. They were divided into needs theories and expectancy theory [3]. Theories of needs deal with the needs of people and the resulting shortage, which is a key motive in the undertaken actions [12]. The driving force of specific actions are the internal needs of people. Man's behaviour strives to meet those needs or reduce deprivation (dissatisfaction). Individuals will behave in such a manner as to meet the activated need [23].

Maslow wrote: "I am motivated when I feel thirst, longing, wish or happiness." The author linked motivation with the aforementioned human conditions but did not manage to distinguish a state that precisely defined the state of motivation [20]. The content theory includes Maslow's needs content theory [20] Alderfer's ERG (existence relatedness and growth) theory [2], Herzberg's two-factor motivation-hygiene theory [8] or McClell's needs trichotomy theory [21]. Alderfer's research showed that the needs identified by Maslow can exist simultaneously and be met, which leads to subjective well-being [2]. Herzberg's motivation-hygiene theory [8], unlike previous concepts, does not focus on the needs but on factors determining job satisfaction. There is a strong correlation between job satisfaction and work results. In turn, McClelland's concept assumes that a person feels all the needs at the same time. Individual needs have different levels of intensity. The one that is most strongly felt has dominant significance and motivates the individual to specific actions. Achieving other goals is of marginal importance to him.

The following theories can be included in the expectancy theory: the theory of Vroom's VIE (valence-instrumentality-expectancy theory) [26], Adams' equity theory, and Skinner's instrumentality theory. The concept of expectations was first formulated by Vroom. It was included in the VIE (valence-instrumentality-expectancy theory). Expectancy theory was developed by Lawler and Porter [24]. Researchers emphasise that employee satisfaction and achievements can be closely related, namely: higher performance at work can lead to greater satisfaction [24]. They identified two variables that affect the achievement of results: ability and role perceptions. Another theory included in the theory of the process is Adams' equity theory in which the main assumption is that employees compare the ratio of their outcomes to their inputs [1].

According to Nieżurawska J., motivation is the force that exists in or influences a person—that is, it stimulates and controls one's behaviour. Motivating is a managerial process that influences the behaviour of employees. Influencing by the creation of enticing or coercive situations, with the use of specific material, non-material incentives, and coercive measures [28].

In research on the essence of motivation, it can be stated that *motivation aims at making people want to work*. Therefore, in the process of motivating employees, it is necessary to take groups of material and non-material motivators into account [28].

The literature on the subject provides many examples of the division of motivation instruments. The authors of these books follow Armstrong M., dividing the instruments of motivation into material and non-material (Figure 3.1). The instruments of material motivation were divided into instruments of financial and non-financial motivation [36, 28].

The monograph adopts a conventional division into traditional and modern approaches to employee motivation. In the literature on the subject, we can find a division into traditional approach to motivating and modern approach to motivating [5]. Some researchers understand the traditional approach to motivation as remuneration and prestige, often supplemented with meaning, creation, challenge, property, and identity. And the modern approach identifies ways of encouraging employees to be more productive and happy at the same time [5]. Traditional motivation, equated with challenges and stimulation and defined as a conscious and deliberate influencing of employees in order to optimally achieve motivator's goals, can be found at work [11].

Concepts based on the traditional approach have undoubtedly made a creative contribution to understanding the phenomenon of work motivation, its sources and mechanisms. The identified needs and expectations, however, did not take into account the diversity and complexity of the contemporary organisational environment created, among others, by the dynamic development of information technologies, demographic changes (aging societies), social changes (new behaviour patterns), including generational changes (new needs and expectations, aspirations, and priorities regarding life and work). The traditional approach, therefore, becomes of little use in solving problems in terms of motivating employees faced by contemporary organisations. The modern approach places a much stronger emphasis on the role of loyalty and engagement contained in the labour resources structure. In particular, the age diversity forces a new perspective on the role of work in human life (work that gives a sense of happiness also in private life), the balance between private life and work, and the role of various types of non-wage benefits.

Taking up the issues of modern concepts of motivating, taking into account generational diversity, stems mainly from cognitive motives but also has practical justification. A possibly comprehensive presentation of not only traditional solutions in the field of motivation, but most of all modern concepts, such as: the concept of work-life balance, cafeteria systems, and the hygge concept, may influence the creation of motivation system solutions, which effectively use these concepts in the process of employee management in various ages.

3.2 Profile of Generation Z

Knowledge about the functioning of generations can be effectively used by employers who, by building good relations with employees and responding to their needs, contribute to the creation of the corporate community. By analysing the available information, they can read the communication from employees more effectively. When choosing a management method, employers should take into account intergenerational differences, individualise motivational techniques, and use new concepts of motivation. When describing generations, one must accept the use of some kind of generalisation in order to highlight specific features that characterise a given group. However, it is important that already at the beginning of the publication, our conviction that there are exceptions in every generation is clearly stated; and the features that we consider typical for a given generation are most often revealed in statistical research.

In the subject literature, we can encounter a division of generations into the following categories: traditionalists (born between 1925–1945), Baby

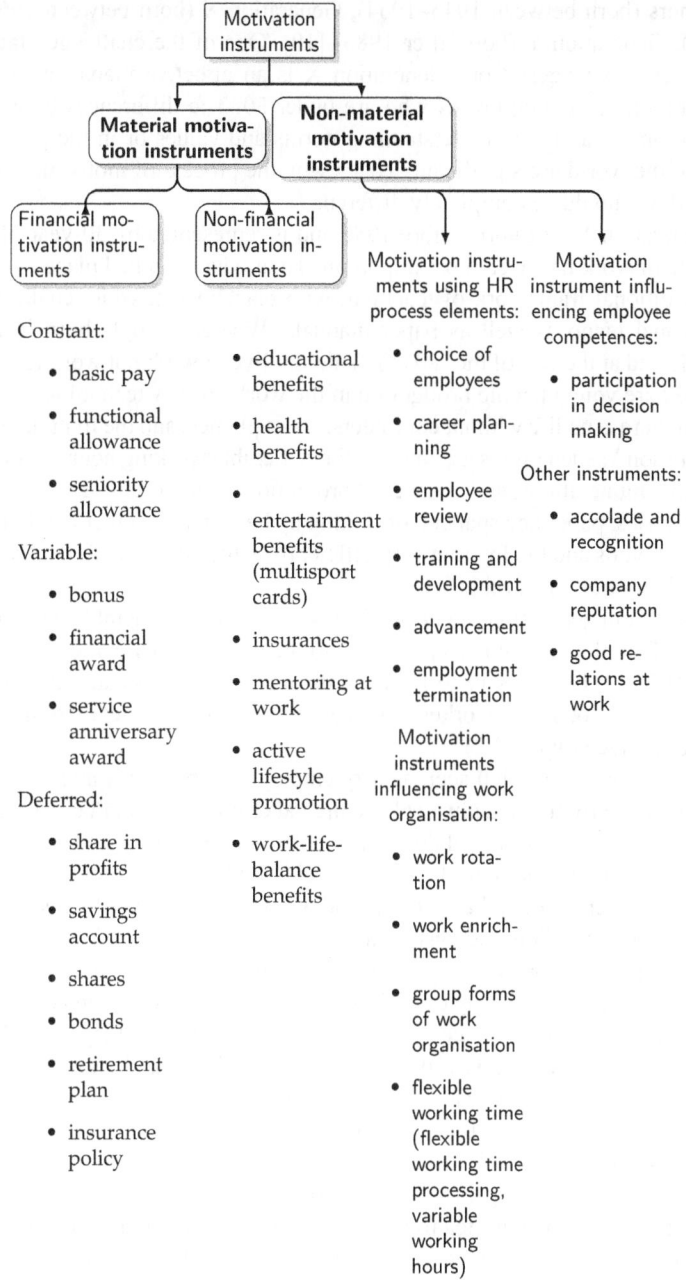

Figure 3.1 Classification of motivation instruments.

Source: own elaboration on the basis of Armstrong, M., 2006, Employee Reward, Chartered Institute of Personnel and Development.

Boomers (born between 1946–1964), Generation X (born between 1965–1980), Generation Y (born after 1980) [10]. One of the challenges faced by modern managers from Generation X is an effective management of Generation Y, i.e. employees who are under 30. The differences between Generation X and Y in understanding norms and values or in the perception of the world are significant. That's why the process of motivating and rewarding should be completely different.

Generation X was born before 1980 and is represented by 30-year-olds, for whom work has been most important. Their education had place within the traditional framework of teaching, with blackboards, white chalk, the traditional piano as well as paper manuals. Whereas people born in the middle and at the end of the '80s (Ys), do not live to work but work to live.

They are young people brought up in the world of new technologies, for whom there is no life without computers, smart phones, and the Internet. For Generation Y, such things as, among others, flexible working hours, results-related remunerations, and chances of promotion are important. They do not use libraries, paper newspapers, or writing by hand. On the other hand, they use keyboards and the Internet very efficiently, where they can find answers to all their questions (Table 3.1).

Apart from generations mentioned above, we need to remember about the group of employees who has just come to the market—Generation Z (born after 1995). It is necessary to focus on them right now—because they will soon become conscious workers with certain salary requirements from their employers (see Figure 3.2).

Generation Z are often seen as lazy employees who aren't interested in any precise activities and physical and mental effort—they don't create anything new, don't protest, and don't have any opinion. Mobile and computer are their communication tools, so they feel "blind" without online connection. Not understanding their attitude and way of thinking by future employers can cause conflicts and clashes in a team.

Only implementation of a cooperation model between employer and Generation Z with precisely established remuneration system can be a solution to an effective and successful team work. To sum up, they should be motivated by benefits that influence work-life balance and allow them to achieve goals in diverse teams [6]. The next important tool is matching the proper flexible system to the needs and wants of Generation Z.

The mentality of Zs is different—they don't need contingent pay for teams, because they represent a generation of only children, individuals, who have problems with teamwork. They constitute a group of most individualistic experts. The freedom is a significant value for them, fun at work, willingness to change here and now. They are more mobile than Ys and expect flexibility from the employer, including such aspects as place, time, and form of work, as well as form of remuneration.

Table 3.1 Generation differences.

Traditionalists (1925–45)	Baby Boomers (1946–64)	Generation X (1965–80)	Generation Y 1 (1981–99)	Generation Z (1995–ongoing)
Priorities: loyalty, focusing on history, anxiousness	Priorities: optimism, a hierarchy of values and life strategy, stabilisation	Priorities: carefulness, interest in innovation, but based on quantitative data	Priorities: life around media and flash, participation in experiments, lifelong learning, relative closeness of peers	Priorities: being global, social, visual, and technological. The employer should provide them sufficient visual and acoustical privacy through physical separation or enclosure. They require a special space to work: equipped with appropriate technology and communication support tools, with Wi-Fi, convenient access to electricity, video, fixed and mobile whiteboards, monitor arms, and trackable surfaces. The space should reflect the personality, image, and brand of the organisation.

(Continued)

Table 3.1 (Continued)

Traditionalists (1925–45)	Baby Boomers (1946–64)	Generation X (1965–80)	Generation Y 1 (1981–99)	Generation Z (1995–ongoing)
At work: worship of heritage, resistance to changes, a method "through trial and error", unnecessary communications, pension claim	At work: interest of development and career, money as a value, need of recognition and prestige (function, post, own office), resistance to changes at work = a loss of own position, difficulties in pulling together in turbulent environment, occasional communications, development only when influences on promotion or salary rise, well-deserved pension	At work: change-orientated, changeable career (every few years), award for progress at work means "freedom" in decision-making and management, being always on the go, relax when retired, need of regular communications (different forms), self-development (courses) as a source of career planning	At work: a few tasks made simultaneously (a few careers) choice of work that is only interesting and in accordance with interests. Work is not the most important as being in different projects/tasks. Requirement of feedback and constant learning, lack of retirement plan.	At work: they are the most connected, educated, and sophisticated generation ever. In general, they are characterised by: • appreciation for order and structure, • strong work ethic, • value sense of predictability in their lives. Work behaviours: • may value practical career choices, • less developed face-to-face social and conflict-resolution skills, • leaders with online collaboration, • susceptible to distractions. They will favour a "legible" planning layout with clear circulation, visual access, and obvious intent of space. They also need space for mentoring, heads-down focus on work and blended online or face-to-face collaboration.

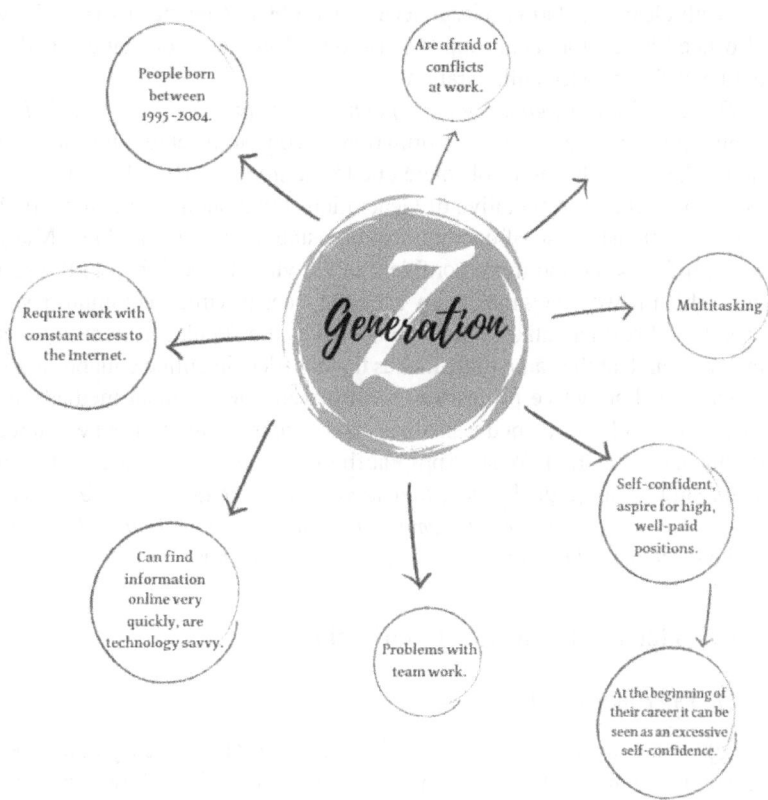

Figure 3.2 Profile of Generation Z.
Source: own research.

Priorities: being global, social, visual, and technological. The employer should provide them sufficient visual and acoustical privacy through physical separation or enclosure. They require special space to work: equipped with appropriate technology and communication support tools, with Wi-Fi, convenient access to electricity, video, fixed and mobile whiteboards, monitor arms and trackable surfaces. The space should reflect the personality, image, and brand of the organisation. At work, they are the most connected, educated, and sophisticated generation ever. In general, they are characterised by appreciation for order, structure, strong work ethics, and value a sense of predictability in their lives.

Work behaviours: may value practical career choices, less developed face-to-face social and conflict-resolution skills, leaders with online collaboration, and are susceptible to distractions. They will favour a "legible" planning layout with clear circulation, visual access, and obvious intent of space. They also need space for mentoring, heads-down focus on work, and blended online or face-to-face collaboration.

The Zs value independence and openness to change because the life they know moves very fast; new information is constantly emerging, and the lion's share of it becomes obsolete due to the influx of new data. It is difficult to meet a representative of Generation Z without a phone in hand. A Z makes intensive use of communication using modern technology. Many of them feel safer and more confident in the virtual world than in the real one, which is why they make new acquaintances in virtual communities—friends and partners alike. This attitude makes it difficult for them to work in a team and, at the same time, makes them leaders in online collaboration.

They lead an active professional and private life in social media, they carefully build social media profiles, and "pamper" their Internet image (Snapchat, Instagram, WhatsApp, Facebook, TikTok). They are global in social and technological terms, *they lead a lush virtual life, modern technologies are an inseparable element of their daily functioning. They are always online and in constant contact with their friends.*

3.3 Modern instruments of motivation

3.3.1 The concept of hygge

Hygge is a peaceful, stress-free, and stimulating way of being in a given situation and in society [4]. It is mostly considered positive; however, there are drawbacks to it as well. Those include social control, abandoning necessity, conflicts, and exclusions of those who do not conform [17].

"Hygge" comes from Scandinavia, and it has gained popularity in Europe, America, and Asia. "Hygge" for the Danes means cosiness, comfort, and joy [17]. The concept affects the conditions and the way the Danes live. In Better Life Index [27], Denmark achieves good results in various fields of life, both social and economic. The society has a strong sense of community and a high level of citizen engagement. The inhabitants maintain balance between their private and professional lives. They enjoy free education [In Denmark, 81% of the population aged 25–64 graduated from secondary education, which is above the OECD average (74%); 82% of women and only 79% of men graduated from secondary education], build tighter social relations, and the average lifespan (81 years) is one year longer than the OECD average [27]. The Danes are satisfied with their lives [The Danes are generally happier with their lives than the average OECD citizen. On a scale of 0 to 10, they rank their life satisfaction at 7.5, which is over the

OECD average of 6.5]. The socio-economic conditions mentioned above contributed to the development of the concept of hygge in the following manner [18].

A Danish professor, Jeppe Trolle Linnet, described hygge as a style of social interaction connected with cultural values. Black and Bodkaer think likewise, seeing hygge as a particular type of social interaction [4] which should be safe and made between people with whom spending time is enjoyable [16].

According to Linnet, hygge works well in private life as well as in commercial settings [19]. In the latter one, hygge can be applied in most of the human resources management areas, but also in the way the enterprise operates in the business environment. The main areas where hygge can be implemented include: motivating the employees, work organisation, but also issues related to the structures within the organisation or business activities (Figure 3.3) [16].

Hygge in the commercial setting is characterised by the presence of greenery whose aim is to relax and calm down the employees during their work. Another need connected with work is egalitarianism and transparency at the workplace, which translates to equality of all employees and transparency of motivating and remuneration policies. Fair play and lack of aggressive behaviours is yet another need accounted for in the pyramid of employees' needs carried out according to the concept of hygge.

The organisational culture of a company which operates according to the concept of hygge is based on mutual trust, teamwork, transparency of actions and decisions, as well as chill, liberty, and spontaneity. Hygge also

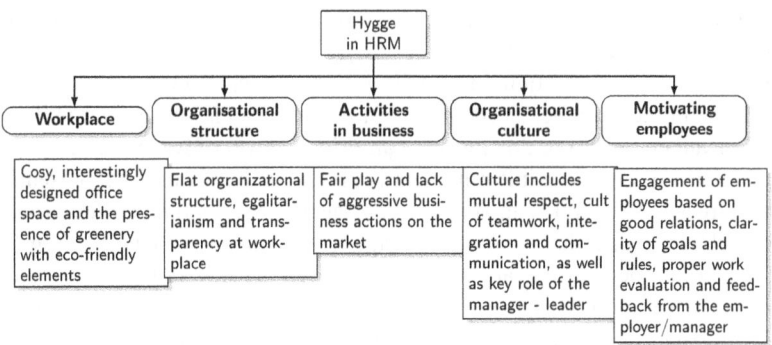

Figure 3.3 Hygge in human resources management.

Source: Iveta Ludviga, Joanna Nieżurawska, Carla Pereira, and Nelson Duarte, "New Ways of Motivation in The Workplace—Hygge: Differences Between Generations and Countries," Proceedings of the 37th International Business Information Management Association (IBIMA), ISBN: 978-0-9998551-6-4, 30–31 May 2021, Cordoba, Spain, p 5388–5395.

means appropriate working conditions, which includes a place where a team can eat lunch or have a coffee break.

Hygge in the workplace develops teamwork and brainstorming. Employees look for solutions together. The structure in such an enterprise is flat, which directly improves communication and reduces the distance between colleagues.

Enterprises implementing hygge will also be recognised by introducing *greenery into the workplace*. Plants relax and calm employees while they perform their duties.

It is important to create a cosy office space, equipped with not only the necessary supplies but also with abundant greenery, good lighting, and surrounding oneself with personal items—such as a favourite mug on the desk [13]. The need is also visible in creating a cosy and modernly designed office space which is dominated by the colours of nature: earth (brown and green) and the sky (blue).

Hygge at workplace is a style aimed at teamwork which includes brainstorming, shared problem-solving, conversations, as well as project meetings. According to hygge, the organisational structure of an enterprise should be flat, which fosters transparency and better communication. According to the concept of hygge, motivating the employees is achieved by increasing their engagement thanks to clear and precise goals, proper employee evaluation, and consistent feedback from the employer/manager (Figure 3.3).

3.3.2 The concept of cafeteria

The concept of remuneration is ambiguous and could mean, e.g., salary (in a narrow sense), or both financial and non-financial incentives (in a broad sense). Increasing flexibility is a tool to motivate employees through salaries. Flexible remuneration, in its narrow sense, means adjusting its level to changes in the level accepted as criteria for them being set up. Variability can mean an upward or downward change in the level of wages [22].

In a broad sense, flexible remuneration refers to the system. It represents an increase of flexibility in adapting to change micro- and macro-environmental conditions, that is possible during mitigating or reducing law regulations (e.g., decreasing rate of employees who are covered by collective labour agreement). It involves also a greater flexibility in creating a structure of packages and each component of this remuneration system.

There are different flexible remuneration conceptions: wages for the effects, payment-by-achievement, payment for skills/competencies, payment based on market research, and cafeteria systems [22].

The idea of flexible remuneration systems refers to both benefits for employees and non-financial incentives obtained as part of the cafeteria. In literature, cafeteria is equivalent to flexible benefits system [3]. This way of understanding the essence of flexible salary systems seems too narrow, as it refers only to one manifestation of flexible payment systems.

American literature often mentions the concept of flexible payroll which is defined as a form of cafeteria which allows employees to be responsible for some health and care services in the form of tax advances being drawn from salary for this purpose.

Cafeteria remuneration has developed mainly in the US, where the salaries are relatively high. The set value is predetermined. Its aim is to meet the needs and wants of individuals. It gives them the opportunity to select the elements which are the most desired by the employees. All of the above mentioned components give the system a participatory dimension. The choice and application of non-financial rewards is determined mainly by cultural factors, both connected with company's and society's culture. Thus, cafeteria is a flexible system where the employees are actively involved in creating their own remuneration package. The basic difference between cafeteria and remuneration package is that the former is chosen by the employee at their discretion, and the latter is imposed.

According to Nieżurawska J, Karaszewska H., and Dziadkiewicz A., the access to each particular element of cafeteria should be well known, fully accepted, and presented in a clear and understandable way to each employee. However, leaving the choice to the employee does not entail complete freedom, as it should be emphasised that it is the employer who decides what privileges and of what value are to be presented to the employee [22].

It is necessary to update all remuneration factors, e.g., every year. Their proportion in total package can also be changed. The procedure of using the service consists in free creation of menu of attractive benefits, where the specific offer, expressed in the terms of money or points form, is at the employee's disposal.

The possibility of choosing the benefits is a perfect solution in cases connected with fitting the benefits to personal needs, especially in those enterprises that provide employment to a significantly demographically diverse profile of employees. Enterprises highly interested in implementing this kind of remuneration are: innovative, rapidly growing, showing respect to employees, and allowing them a lot of leeway and treating them as individuals.

In Poland, there are only few enterprises or selected professional groups where cafeteria systems are effective. First of all, they include companies which meet the basic needs such as financial security. Thus, the priority managerial task is to identify the target group—mostly managers and top management—which can take advantage of the cafeteria system [22]. The mentality of Zs is different—they don't need contingent pay for teams, because they represent a generation of only children, individuals, who have problems with teamwork. They constitute a group of most individualistic experts. Freedom is a significant value for them, as well as fun at work and willingness to change here and now. They are more mobile than Ys and expect flexibility from the employer, including such aspects as place, time, and form of work, as well as form of remuneration. It is expected that generation Z will take multitasking to a brand new level. Challenges are what they love most. Their attitude can be summarised by the phrase "they don't represent the future, they create it."

3.3.3 The concept of work-life balance

One of the reasons for the increase in stress level or professional and family conflicts may be *the imbalance between work and private life. Overwork has a negative effect on personal relationships and negatively affects our social roles*. It also leads to the fact that overworked people neglect their relationships, not having the time and energy to care for them. Among people suffering from imbalance, one can observe a decrease in well-being, depressive states, and seeking consolation and relief in stimulants (alcohol, drugs). Mental and physical fatigue makes the activities that we have previously undertaken with pleasure become tedious and frustrating for us. *The excess of duties does not allow us to maintain a healthy distance and create space for regeneration.* Unequal time-sharing between private and professional life contributes to low self-esteem and creates the impression that our life is chaotic and we have no control over it.

Better Life Index is a tool that measures the hours spent on non-work activities (sleep, meals, relaxation, passions, family time). The average BLI score is 15 hours, which allows to determine at what level individual countries find work-life balance. *Among others, Denmark and Belgium are high in the ranking. In these countries, employees spend about 15.9 hours on activities that go beyond their official duties [30].*

In the *Better Life Index*, Denmark performs well in many areas of life, both social and economic. Society shows a *strong sense of community* and a high level of *civic involvement*. Citizens maintain a work-life balance, enjoy free education, build closer social relationships, and life expectancy is one year longer than the OECD average [30].

As Armstrong [3] explains, work-life balance (WLB) is a modern concept of motivating, consisting of various types of organisational practices and programmes, which actively helps employees achieve success at work and home.

According to this management philosophy, maintaining harmony between various spheres of human functioning should lead to an increase in the level of satisfaction with both professional and private life. The core elements of the work-life balance concept usually include flexibility in the workplace, health and beauty, cultural initiatives, and community involvement (Figure 3.4).

In the literature on the subject, work-life balance is often combined with the need for self-realisation. Striving for self-realisation is characteristic of national cultures with a higher degree of individualism and a small power distance. Hence, this concept is more widespread in the management of organisations in countries with a higher level of social development and, therefore, of prosperity. In high-income developed countries, welfare is becoming a standard, and the salary is already high enough for the worker to be able to satisfy also higher-order needs, which include self-fulfilment.

As explained by Geert Hofstede, Gert Jan Hofstede, and Michael Minkov, in national cultures with a high level of individualism, self-realisation is the most important goal of each individual. Your position in society is determined by your achievements and determination to meet your own needs and aspirations. Employees feel a greater need to have free time to deal with personal and family matters and expect freedom to choose their own approach to the job, i.e., increased flexibility in the workplace. This requires changes in the methods of managing employee capital and creates the need to adapt the employment law to the realities of the modern labour market.

In the 1980s and 1990s, work-life programmes were more often offered by enterprises in more developed countries. Initially, these programmes are

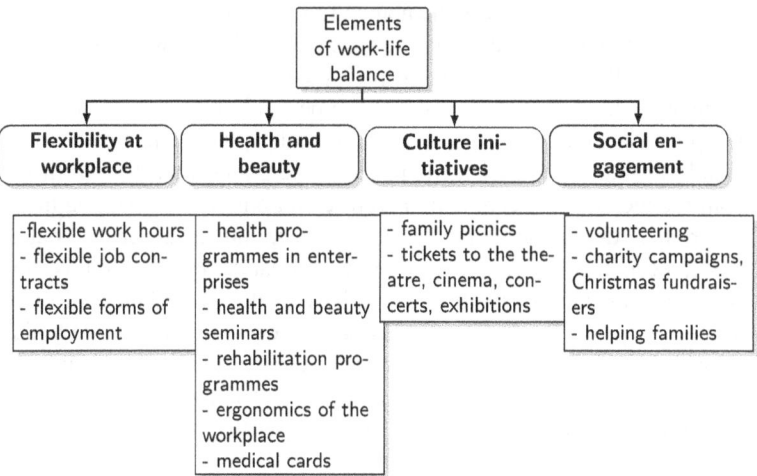

Figure 3.4 Elements of *work-life balance*.

Source: own study.

mainly used by women with children; however, this changes over time. As N. R. Lockwood writes, work-life programmes are now offered regardless the gender and also recognise other commitments as determinants of balance. This does not mean, however, that they do not need to be adjusted to the gender, age, or education of employees. These are important criteria for differentiating people's needs and goals.

It is worth adding that specialists claim that currently high expectations towards employers regarding work-life programmes are shown especially by people born in the 1980s and later. Happiness for them is tantamount to achieving a harmonious and satisfying life in all areas of functioning. They need more time to care for their loved ones and fulfil their own aspirations and expect the possibility of leaving the working day in a crisis [14].

As can be seen, the increase in the popularity of the concept of work-life balance in employee management was caused by interrelated economic, social, and cultural changes in the ways of functioning of systems such as national economies. This can be summarised in the words of Walt Whitman Rostov, an outstanding researcher of social development, who, in his works, illustrates the relationship between the increase in prosperity and the change in the aspirations of generations. According to Rostov, initially, the first generation looks for money; the second one is born with money and seeks social recognition that can be achieved thanks to the position or role played in the family; the third one, born in comfort, looks for the music of life, for which they need more free time—for example, in the form of three-day weekends. In other words, maintaining a work-life balance is becoming more and more important.

Other researchers of social phenomena are of a similar opinion. For example, Toffler points out that economic development breaks with the hard work ethos of the Protestant ethic that is promoted in the second-wave societies, the industrialised economies. During the period of high mass consumption that precedes the stage of post-industrial society, the welfare state concept usually grows in popularity. Members of the public want to benefit more from the income they earn and, therefore, not only are demanding that the government define the scope of social welfare and social security but also start to keep its promises. Society ceases to treat the increase in investment in the development of modern technology as the overriding goal of economic policy, which it is to be subject to and devote to in order to build an industrial civilisation. As a consequence, an increasing number of members of society no longer want to live a puritan lifestyle based on the principles of rational management and saving, especially as they see the so-called elect of the nation overflowing with luxury.

The shaping of a new approach to work characteristic of post-industrial societies is also favoured by the development of a knowledge-based economy, more flexible ways of organising work in conjunction with the decentralisation of management and the development of information and communication technology facilitating remote work. Members of post-industrial societies who are better educated and equipped with modern technologies are more efficient, able to cooperate and share knowledge, have greater autonomy in action, and the ability to manage their own development. Consequently, they earn more and work shorter hours, more often at home.

Having more free time, they spend it on self-fulfilment, pleasing themselves, engaging in the life of various communities they create, and working for their own use. They treat work for their own use and their communities as recreation and self-fulfilment. Therefore, they will be more willing to choose flexible part-time employment in order to maintain a work-life balance and be able to manage their work more independently.

At the end of this part of the article, the results of the OECD research, which are part of the project to develop the OECD Better Life Index, will be presented in order to show the context in which research on work-life balance is conducted by international institutions. They are usually part of a broader indicator of well-being or quality of life.

According to the OECD, work-life balance is about being able to combine family commitments, leisure and work, including both paid and unpaid work. Across OECD countries, the average time spent on leisure and personal care by full-time employed people ranges from around 14 to 16.5 hours per day. Full-time employed men enjoy 30 minutes more leisure and personal care time relative to women, while the young and old spend 50 and 25 minutes more than the middle-aged, respectively.

When considering both paid and unpaid working time together, women work, on average, 25 minutes longer per day than men do. Gender gaps are largest in Italy, Spain, Estonia, Greece, and Hungary, where women spend over one hour per day more than men in total work. By contrast, men in Norway, New Zealand, and the Netherlands spend lightly more time in total work than women.

Average satisfaction with time use, measured on a 0–10 scale, never exceeds 8 and can be as low as 5.6. In the 29 OECD countries, the highest ratings were found in Denmark (7.8), Finland and Mexico (7.7), and the Netherlands (7.5), and the lowest in Hungary (6.3), Greece (6.1), and Turkey (5.6). As mentioned above, middle-aged people are consistently the least satisfied with their time used. The OECD average satisfaction with time used is 7 for people aged 16–29 and 7.4 for people aged 50 and above, compared to 6.4 for people aged 30–49 [30], pages 158–165.

According to Majewska and Nieżurawska, the respondents, regardless of their belonging to the distinguished groups, declared that WLB solutions are important to them. Offering WLB facilitation programmes by companies is most important for members of the BB generation, especially women, and least important for men and members of Generation Y. As expected, it is more important for women that companies offer them solutions that help them reconcile work and private life. In Poland, classified as one of the countries with a male culture with a significant power distance, such a situation is undoubtedly influenced by the still-dominant traditional family model and the depreciation of the role of women in the labour market and in deciding about their fate [29].

The results of the research show, therefore, that employers do not make it easier for older workers who already require a different work organisation to maintain a work-life balance. This is worrying as it may be one of the reasons for their decision to withdraw from the labour market, especially since we are dealing with growing labour shortages in Poland. As in other developed countries, it is caused by the ageing population [29].

The same applies to employees with primary education who mostly perform manual work that the young generation would not necessarily undertake even in the event of a lack of livelihood. This, in turn, is related to the fact that prosperity makes you lazy. This is reflected, inter alia, in the fact that young people in countries with a higher level of prosperity do not want to study medicine or other fields that require more effort from them.

Thus, the results of the research showed that it is necessary to increase the degree of adjustment of WLB programmes to the needs of employees. This would make it easier for employees to cope with work-life balance and increase their job satisfaction. The most satisfied with the WLB programmes offered to them are the representatives of the Z generation for both genders, i.e., the youngest employees and men with higher education. This is due to the fact that employees who are on the threshold of their professional career choose the job that offers WLB packages, or simply, in their opinion, the benefits in the field of balance are sufficient for them at that moment. In the future, it may change. Generation Z in the current situation is focused on achieving professional success and developing their competencies. Their main goal is to "earn money", for example, to be able to become independent and move away from their parents, or to spend the earned money on a hobby. Hence, in the case of the representatives of Generation Z, the gap in the effectiveness of the incentive system turned out to be the smallest.

During the COVID-19 pandemic, expectations regarding remote work and flexible working hours have certainly decreased. Generation Z took advantage of the possibility of working online. However, Generations Y and X with children who use online learning have been very critical of this form of work. Further research and new forms of incentive solutions in the event of a pandemic are needed in this regard [29].

Other studies conducted by Nieżurawska among Polish students representing Generation Z proved that the concept of work-life balance is important to the younger generation. *The implementation of benefits and management methods that balance private and professional life in companies has a positive effect on the motivation of the employed personnel.* A satisfied employee is not only *more productive* but is also *willing to stay longer in the company.* Research results show that flexibility at work is the most important for the youngest generation. Another important motivator for Zs are health and beauty programmes. On the other hand, Zs do not pay attention (or only to a negligible extent) to family picnics, free tickets, volunteer programmes, and helplines [28].

3.3.4 Motivation and employee engagement and loyalty

Engagement includes expressing yourself through work [33], which is associated with initiative and learning. Rich, Lepine, and Crawford argue that involvement occurs when *members of an organisation use their potential and energy in physical, cognitive, and emotional activities.* The American Society of Human Resource Management (USA) describes engagement as binding employees to work, dedication to the organisation, and loyalty to the employer [44].

Work engagement is described as the psychological presence of an employee in his or her work position [31]. Work engagement is also defined as the degree of work absorption [34]. Employee engagement is also referred to as "work engagement," which refers to how enthusiastic an individual employee is about his or her employment [35].

Personal engagement and personal disengagement were described by Kahn [31]. He described personal engagement as the use of members of the company in their employee roles, and personal disengagement as a physical, cognitive, or emotional withdrawal from employee roles [31].

Kahn was the first to argue that people who are emotionally engaged in their work invest positive emotional and cognitive energy in achieving their goals [36].

According to Rich, Lepine, and Crawford, engagement happens when members of an organisation put their potential and resources into physical, cognitive, and emotional action [37]. Employee engagement is described by the American Society of Human Resource Management as an employee's relationship with their job, commitment to the company, and loyalty to their employer [37]. Given its clear connection to important attitudinal and behavioural results, a deeper understanding of the organisational engagement process is especially useful [38, 39, 37]. When considering the effect of policies on work engagement [40] and reflecting on multiple policies, the essence of the temporal change will be significant [41]. In addition, there is evidence in the literature that this organisational-level engagement mediates the relationship between motivational activities and organisational performance [42] (see Table 3.2).

Table 3.2 Defining employee engagement in literature.

Author and source	Type of engagement	Definition
Kahn	Member of organisation	Use of the member of organisation
CIPD	Employee engagement	Includes measures of influence that employers have over employees
Harter et al.	Employee engagement	Participation, satisfaction, and enthusiasm of employees
Macey'a et al.	Employee engagement	The personal goal of the person performing the task, concentration of energy in a way that is visible to other employees by taking the initiative
Armstrong	Employee engagement	A situation in which employees feel positive and enthusiastic about the workplace
Juchnowicz	Basis of employee engagement	Willingness to give up personal goals in favour of an organisation or professional activity while being ready to take responsibility in conditions of independent action and in non-standard situations
Juchnowicz	Employee engagement	A special attitude at work is manifested: above-average readiness to act, in which the interests of the organisation are as important as the individual's own interests. The attitude is expressed in a passion for action, identification with the company (employees believe in the success of the organisation, expressing opinions about the organisation), and the willingness to stay in the organisation
Kenexa Company	Employee engagement	The level of motivation of employees to contribute to the success of the organisation and to make extraordinary effort (additional time, intellectual effort, dedication to achieve the goals of the organisation)
Institute for Employment Studies	Employee engagement	Positive attitude of the employee towards the organisation and its values. A committed employee is aware of the business context and of cooperation with employees to improve their performance
The Gallup Organisation	Employee engagement	Engaging in and enthusiasm for work
Rich, Lepine, and Crawford	Employee engagement	Members of the organisation use their potential and energy in physical, cognitive, and emotional activities

Table 3.3 Sample employee loyalty questionnaire.

	1	2	3	4	5
1. I defend the good name of this company	☐	☐	☐	☐	☐
2. I feel proud of my work.	☐	☐	☐	☐	☐
3. I strongly feel that I'm part of this company.	☐	☐	☐	☐	☐
4. I keep professional secrets.	☐	☐	☐	☐	☐
5. My company matters greatly to me.	☐	☐	☐	☐	☐
6. My company is an authority for me.	☐	☐	☐	☐	☐
7. I'm a loyal employee.	☐	☐	☐	☐	☐
8. I intend to go on working for this organisation.	☐	☐	☐	☐	☐

Note: 1 → I fully disagree 2 → I don't agree 3 → I'm not sure 4 → I agree 5 → I fully agree

The term loyalty is present in many areas, from management sciences to psychology, sociology, philosophy, pedagogy and even law; considering such a wide range of domains, the term loyalty must be read depending on the context. Considering the interdisciplinary nature of the concept, it cannot be classified and interpreted unambiguously. The word loyal comes from the Latin word legalis—meaning lawful [45].

Some authors argue loyalty stems from extrinsic reward, which assertedly produces organisation stability, and contributes to the success of an enterprise [46].

On the basis of research carried out by Kets de Vries, the characteristics of a loyal employee have been distinguished. These are: concern for the good of the company, attachment to the workplace, reliability, diligence in performing tasks, readiness to unconditionally comply with the rules and standards applicable in the company. The author also emphasises the importance of interpersonal factors in the process of creating an atmosphere of trust and a sense of common aspirations and goals at work [45]. Table 3.3 shows an example of a loyalty questionnaire.

Bibliography

[1] Adams J.S. (1963), *Towards an understanding of inequity*, The Journal of Abnormal and Social Psychology, 67(5), 422–431.

[2] Alderfer C.P. (1969), *An empirical test of a new theory of human needs*, Organizational Behavior and Human Performance nr, 4(2), s. 142–175.

[3] Armstrong M. (2006), *Employee Reward*, Chartered Institute of Personnel and Development, pp. 55–66.

[4] Black, B., Bodkaer, M. (2018), *Hygge racism: noget som man nok urger mere end man taenker over. A qualitative study of well-intentioned racism*, 9.

[5] Damij N., Levnajić Z., Rejec Skrt V., Suklan J. (2015), *What motivates us for work? Intricate web of factors beyond money and prestige*, PloS One, 10(7), e0132641. https://doi.org/10.1371/journal.pone.0132641

[6] Dziadkiewicz A., Kłos M. (2013), *Tworzenie zespołów różnorodnych w przedsiebiorstwach zorientowanych na design*, Przedsiebiorczość I Zarzadzanie, 14(12, cz. 2 Zarzadzanie w XXI wieku.´ Menedzer innowacyjnej organizacji. Cześć II), 361–374.

[7] Goić S. (2017), *Employees older than 50 on Croatian labour market: Need for a new approach*, Journal of Human Resource Management, 2, 1–11.

[8] Herzberg F.M., Mausner B.B., Snyderman B.B. (1959), *The motivation to work*, New York and London: AUFL, s. 126–128.

[9] Hitka M., Lorincova S., Pajtinkov Bartakov G., Lizbetinova L., Starchon P., Li C., Zaborova E., Markova T., Schmidtova J., Mura L., et al. (2018), *Strategic tool of human resource management for operation of SMEs in the wood-processing industry*, BioResources, 13, 2759–2774.

[10] Jamka B. (2012), *Czynnik ludzki we współczesnym przedsiebiorstwie: zasób czy kapitał? Od zarzadzania kompetencjami do zarzadzania róz norodnościa.* Warszawa: Oficyna Wolters Kluwer business.

[11] Juchnowicz M. (2012), [in Polish] *Zaangaz owanie pracowników*, Sposoby oceny i motywowania, Warszawa: PWE, p. 121.

[12] Karaś R. (2003), *Teorie motywacji w zarzadzaniu*, Akademia Ekonomiczna, s.14.

[13] *Hygge-scandinavian philosophy of happiness: Use it in your company!* (2016), Harvard Business Review, 20 December. www.hbrp.pl/b/hygge-skandy-nawska-filozofia-szczescia-wykorzystaj-ja-w-swojej-firmie/tVClx3fi.

[14] Nieżurawska J. (2020), *Motivating in Managing Generational Diversity*, Poland: CDEWO.

[15] Kooij D., Jansen P.G.W., Dikkers J.E., De Lange A. (2010), *The influence of age on the associations between HR practices and both affective commitment and job satisfaction: A meta-analysis*, Journal of Organizational Behavior, 31, 1111–1136.

[16] Linnet J.T. (2011), Interiority in Consumer Culture, in NA — Advances in Consumer Research Volume 38, eds. Darren W. Dahl, Gita V. Johar, and Stijn M.J. van Osselaer, Duluth, MN: Association for Consumer Research. https://www.acrwebsite.org/volumes/16025/volumes/v38/NA-38

[17] Linnet, J.T. (2011), *Money can't buy me hygge: Danish middle-class consumption, egalitarianism, and the sanctity of inner space*, Social Analysis, 22–24.

[18] Linnet, J.T. (2012), *The social-material performance of cozy interiority*, In Ambiances in Action/Ambiances en acte (s)-International Congress on Ambiances, International Ambiances Network, 403.

[19] Lugosi P. (2009), *The production of hospitable space: Commercial propositions and consumer co-creation in a bar operation*, Space and Culture, 12(4), 396–411.

[20] Maslow A. (1955), *The theory of human motivation*, Psychological Review, s. 370–385.

[21] McClelland D.C., Atkinson, J.W., Clark, R.A., Lowell, E.L. (1953), *The achievement motive*, New York: Appleton-Century-Crofts, s. 262.

[22] Nieżurawska J., Karaszewska H., Dziadkiewicz A. (2016), *Attractiveness of cafeteria systems as viewed by Generation Z*, 18th International Conference on Economics and Human Resource Management, Word Academy of Science Engineering and Technology WASET, London, pp. 1242–1246. 1307–5892. International Journal of Social, Behavioral, Educational, Economic, Busi-

ness and Industrial Engineering EISSN:2010–3778. www.waset.org/publications/10006128.

[23] Penc, J. (2007), *Decyzje i zmiany w organizacji: w poszukiwaniu skutecznych sposobów działania*, Difin, Warszawa, pp. 145–146.

[24] Porter L.W., Lawrer E.E. (1968), *Management Attitiudes and Behavior*, Homewood, IL: Irwin-Dorsey.

[25] Rabl T. (2010), *Age, discrimination, and achievement motives: A study of German employees*, Personnel Review, 39, 448–467.

[26] Vroom V.H. (1964), op. cit., Naylor J.C., Pritchard R.D., Ilgen D.R. (1980), *A Theory of Behavior in Organisations*, New York: Academic Press, s. 194–195.

[27] Source: www.oecdbetterlifeindex.org/de/countries/denmark-de/.

[28] Nieżurawska-Zajac   Joanna   (2020),   *Motywowanie   pracowników zróżnicowanych pokoleniowo*, CeDeWu Warszawa 2020, ss.: 422.

[29] Majewska N.-Z. (2021), *Assessment of effectiveness of work-life balance systems in opinions of women and men*, Proceedings of the 37th International Business Information Management Association (IBIMA), ISBN: 978-0-9998551-6-4, 30–31 May, Cordoba, Spain, pp. 5437–5444.

[30] OECD (2020), *Work-Life Balance, in How's Life? 2020: Measuring Well-Being, Work-Life Balance*, Paris: OECD Publishing. https://doi.org/10.1787/e6597da1-en

[31] Kahn W.A. (1990), *Psychological conditions of personal engagement and disengagement at work*, Academy of Management Journal, 33, 692–724.

[32] Gerard H.S., Meredith J.W., Grant T.S. (2018), *International perspectives on the relationship between leadership and employee engagement*, Academy of Management Annual Meeting Proceedings, Published Online:23 February 2018.

[33] Rothbard N.P. (2001), *Enriching or depleting? The dynamics of engagement in work and family*, Administrative Science Quarterly, 46, 655–684.

[34] Farndale E., Rich B.L. (2018), *Broadening the foci of employee engagement: Definitions, antecedents, and outcomes*, Academy of Management Annual Meeting Proceedings, Published Online: 23 February 2018.

[35] Armstrong M. (2006), *Employee Reward, Chartered Institute of Personnel and Development*.

[36] Rich B.L., Lepine J., Crawford E. (2010), *Job engagement: Antecedents and effect on job performance*, Academy of Management Journal, 53(2), s. 617–635.

[37] Christian M.S., Garza A.S., Slaughter J.E. (2011), *Work engagement: A quantitative review and test of its relations with task and contextual performance*, Personnel Psychology, 64(1), 89–136.

[38] May D.R., Gilson R.L., Harter L.M. (2004), *The psychological conditions of meaningfulness, safety and availability and the engagement of the human spirit at work*, Journal of Occupational and Organisational Psychology, 77(1), 11–37.

[39] Smith J.E.P., Dumas T.L. (2007, August), *Debunking the ideal worker myth: Effects of temporal flexibility & family configuration on engagement*, in *Acad-*

emy of Management Proceedings, Volume 2007, No. 1, Briarcliff Manor, NY 10510: Academy of Management, pp. 1–6.

[40] Perry-Smith J.E., Blum T.C. (2000), *Work-family human resource bundles and perceived firm performance*, Academy of Management Journal, 43, 1107–1117.

[41] Thurgood G., Smith T., Barrick M.R. (2013), *Job design, HR systems, CEO leadership and firm performance: A strategic theory of engagement*, in *Academy of Management Proceedings*, Volume 2013, No. 1, Briarcliff Manor, NY 10510: Academy of Management, p. 11098.

[42] Rich B.L., Lepine J., Crawford E. (2010), *Job engagement: Antecedents and effect on job performance*, Academy of Management Journal, 53(2), s. 617–635.

[43] Kets de Vries M.F. (1994), *The leadership mystique*, Academy of Management Perspectives, 8(3), s.73–89.

[44] Carbone J.H. (1997), *Loyalty: Subversive doctrine?*, Academy of Management Perspectives, 11(3), 80–86.

4 Work values and motivating factors of generation Z—the analysis of empirical research in Poland, Portugal, and Latvia

Iveta Ludviga and Inese Sluka

In this chapter, we present the empirical study about workplace-related values and motivational factors with a special focus on Generation Z.

The nature of work has changed over the last decades. With Gen Z entering the workforce in large numbers, everything about work and business is changing because their work-related needs and values are different. Understanding individuals' work values and motivating factors would help organisations to gain insight into what motivates their workers and create work environments that will enable their employees to be more productive.

This empirical investigation aims to create a new instrument for measuring motivating factors and work values by updating the Minnesota Importance Questionnaire by adding new items related to the contemporary workplace and to test it in the selected European countries Poland, Latvia, and Portugal (n = 1195). Exploratory factor analysis found seven workplace-related value dimensions: achievement, supervision, comfort, altruism, independence, excitement, and technologies. Our results show that the traditional work-related values of the four studied generations are similar. Only three out of seven values are impacted by generation—independence is more important for older generations, while excitement and technologies are more important for younger generations.

4.1 The need for understanding workplace values

Alongside the continuing changing nature of work in the 21st century [1], organisations need to integrate four generations of employees in the workplace [2]. HR professionals (e.g., SHRM, Deloitte) are expressing concern that the needs and expectations of younger generations of employees differ, and therefore, talent acquisition becomes one of the main challenges of the future [3]. Because a high-quality workforce is the most important determinant of business success, these challenges have a direct influence on organisations' competitiveness both today and in the future.

DOI: 10.4324/9781003353935-4

For a growing number of employers, understanding the needs and expectations of employees, especially millennials and the Z generation is crucial—attracting talent requires them to know what exactly they expect from the employer [4]. There is a lot of debate among HR professionals about workplace expectations, and the general belief is that each generation has different ways or so-called models of how they want to build a career [5]. Professionals are thinking about how to update their strategies in order to attract and retain the youth in a company [6]. Moreover, researchers discussing generational differences suggest that individuals of more recent generations have different work-related needs and values than do individuals of older generations, and those values affect career choice [2, 15]. On the other hand, from the candidate's perspective, the problem is that they struggle to find a position that fits their desires and expectations. The extent to which an individual finds a well-fitting occupation represents the individual's overall positive judgement of his or her future life and career and was found to correlate positively with overall life satisfaction [7].

Understanding individual work values and preferences would help organisations to gain insight into what motivates their workers and create work environments that will enable their employees to be more productive [8]. Researchers suggest that shifts in employees' personal work values compel employers to be continuously attentive to changing work requirements and areas of employee skill development [9]. Moreover, an individual's system of beliefs is a key component in the construction and development of individual careers and the career systems of organisations and even societies [10]. Thus, understanding employees' work-related values is important for organisations to design motivating workplaces.

Individuals' work-related needs and values are frequently measured using the Minnesota Importance Questionnaire (MIQ), which includes 20 facets of values grouped in six overarching values (2) or modified and computerised work impotence profiler (WIP-C) developed by [11]. However, both instruments were developed long ago, in the 20th century, and, consequently, do not include some factors important in the contemporary workplace. The nature of work has changed over the last decades and is likely to continue to change [1]. For example, a contemporary work environment is not imaginable without information technologies. Artificial intelligence is going to become more frequent. Organisations and businesses are international and global in nature. Moreover, employees as individuals are changing. For example, analysing the work-related values of Generation Z in Poland, Portugal, and Latvia found that the workplace behaviour of Generation Z employees is radically different from that of older generations' [12]. Researchers report clashing value systems among generations [13] and the innate need for technologies [14]. Generation Z is just entering the workplace, and research about their needs and values is scarce. Still, managers and HR practitioners have realised that "today's generation of young workers is different" ([15] p. 837).

Given these changing contexts of the workplace and continuing challenge to learn what motivates younger generations of individuals on the job, the aim of this research is twofold. First, it aims to update MIQ by including values important for younger generations and test it in selected European countries. Second, to identify whether the work-related values of individuals differ according to demographic variables such as age, gender, employment experience, and generation as they relate to one's suitability for specific work environments. By exploring work-related demands, needs, and values, we aim to identify if younger-generation values differ and answer the question of *how "should" employers treat Generation Z employees? Are their work-related demands, needs, and values different from those of millennials and older generations?*

This chapter is organised as follows. First, the comparison of existing methods for measuring workplace-related values is performed, and deficiencies related to different expectations of employees in the contemporary workplace are identified. Second, the new, updated version of the questionnaire is developed, and workplace-related values are measured in three European countries: Poland, Latvia, and Portugal. Results present the factor analysis and impact of country, age, and generation. Finally, the implications and propositions for future research are discussed.

4.2 Theoretical background for creation of the survey

4.2.1 Work values and the theory of work adjustment

One of the dominant theories concerning the decision-making process involved in occupational choices is dealing with the adjustment of individuals to the specific occupation they have chosen. It is the theory of work adjustment (TWA) which is based on the principle that an individual seeks to achieve and maintain correspondence with his work environment [16] and this person-environment correspondence contributes to job satisfaction and retention with an organisation [17]. Work values relate to objective or psychological state, a relationship, or material condition that one seeks to attain at the workplace [18]. Theory of work adjustment conceptualises work values as aspects of a job that are necessary to ensure job satisfaction [2]. TWA identifies six key values: achievement—conditions that encourage accomplishment and progress; comfort—conditions that encourage lack of stress; status—conditions that provide recognition and prestige; altruism—conditions that foster harmony and service to others; safety—conditions that establish predictability and stability; autonomy—conditions that increase personal control and initiative [19].

According to TWA, the more closely the work environment in the organisation corresponds to the values that a person seeks to satisfy through the work, the more likely it is that the person will perceive the job as satisfying [20]. Similarly [21], states that a person's career anchor is his or her self-concept, consisting of talents and abilities, basic values, and a sense of motives and needs.

The way to operationalize TWA and measure individuals' work-related needs and values is the Minnesota Importance Questionnaire (MIQ), which is designed to provide information about 21 vocationally relevant needs or facets of value. These needs are grouped into six overarching values [22]. Later the original MIQ item wording was slightly modified, and computerised work impotence profiler to measure work values (WIP=C) was developed [11]. McCloy and colleagues also renamed some of the needs (see Table 4.1). Both instruments have proven to be valid in different contexts; however, since developed long ago, MIQ and WIP-C do not include some factors important in the contemporary workplace.

As seen from the table, the titles of work-related needs and values have slightly changed over time. Based on Table 4.1, we also see some limitations of those existent tools—several important aspects of contemporary workplace are not included. Researchers suggest that individuals of more recent generations have different work-related needs and values than do individuals of older generations, and those values affect their job and career choice (e.g., [2, 15, 26]). For example, new technologies are transforming the society and have a serious impact on human values ([29], p. 51). As indicated by SHRM, young people are more willing to work for themselves as contractors, consultants, freelancers, and "taskers" [30]. Employees from younger generations value passion, purpose, flexibility, transparency, collaboration, trust, and autonomy [31]. Further, the differences are discussed from the generational perspective.

4.2.2 *Work values across generations*

Despite the fact that modern history is a source of generational titles, the main trend of contemporary research of historical generations "is cautiously empirical, with very moderate theoretical expectations" ([23] p. 280). While the research on generational differences has continued to grow, there are still questions about whether "generation" is a useful construct [24]; therefore, in this research, "generation" is used only as a reference point. We do not aim to identify differences between generation cohorts but to find out if younger employees have different work-related needs and values and "should" employers treat Generation Z employees differently in today's work environment.

Table 4.1 Comparison of the existing instruments (MIQ and WIP=C items) to measure work-related needs and overarching values.

In my ideal job it is important that (statements adapted from MIQ and WIP-C)	Vocational need MIQ (original) Rounds et al 1981	Work importance profiler (WIP=C) by McCloy et al 1999, p. 74	Value group by Hansen & Leuty, 2012
1 I make use of my abilities	Ability utilisation	Achievement	Achievement
2 the work could give me a feeling of accomplishment	Achievement	Achievement	Achievement
3 I could be busy all the time	Activity	Comfort	Working conditions
4 the job would provide an opportunity for advancement	Working conditions	Status	Recognition
5 I could give directions and instructions to others	Authority	Status	Recognition
6 I would be treated fairly by the company	Company policies and practices	Safety	Support
7 my pay would compare well with that of other workers	Compensation	Comfort	Working conditions
8 my co-workers would be easy to get along with	Co-workers	Altruism	Relationships
9 I could try out my own ideas	Creativity	Authonomy	Independence
10 I could work alone	Independence	Comfort	Working conditions
11 I would never be pressured to do things that go against my sense of right and wrong	Moral values	Altruism	Relationships
12 I could receive recognition for the work I do	Recognition	Status	Recognition
13 I could make decisions on my own	Responsibility	Authonomy	Independence
14 the job would provide for steady employment	Security	Comfort	Working conditions
15 I could do things for other people	Social service	Altruism	Relationships
16 I would be looked up to by others in my company and my community	Social status	Status	Recognition

(*Continued*)

Table 4.1 (Continued)

In my ideal job it is important that (statements adapted from MIQ and WIP-C)	Vocational need MIQ (original) Rounds et al 1981	Work importance profiler (WIP=C) by McCloy et al 1999, p. 74	Value group by Hansen & Leuty, 2012
17 I have supervisors who would back up their workers with management	Supervision— human relations	Safety	Support
18 I would have supervisors who train workers well	Supervision— technical	Safety	Support
19 I could do something different every day	Variety	Comfort	Working conditions
20 the job would have good working conditions	Working conditions	Comfort	Working conditions
21 I could plan my work with little supervision	Authonomy	Authonomy	Independence

Generation is defined as "a group of individuals born and living contemporaneously who have common knowledge and experiences that affect their thoughts, attitudes, values, beliefs and behaviour" ([25] p. 6). According to adherents of a generational perspective of workplace dynamics, workers and employers widely accept the belief that employees bring and transmit their personal values, attitudes, and lifestyle preferences with them into the workplace [26].

There is general agreement about generational titles; however, there is little agreement on the bounding years. The boomers' birth years are reported to begin anywhere from 1946 and to end in 1964, Gen Xers' to begin somewhere from 1965 and to end in 1976, and Gen Yers' to begin from 1977 and end in 1994 [15, 45, 46]. Some sources mention 2001 as the beginning of the Generation Z births, but others consider Gen Z starting the birth year 1995, as the boundaries of the generations are becoming more blurred and vague, and the generations are more characterised by their values than the years of birth [27]. According to [42], the Z generation is the one born between 1994 and 2009, but those born after 2009 represent the Alpha generation.

According to previous studies, coinciding common social events guides the individual values of a generation. Due to different formative events and settings in their past, Boomers, Gen Xers, Gen Yers, and Gen Zers hold different expectations, preferences, and differences in values related to work [28]. For example, new technologies are transforming society and have a serious impact on human values ([29] pp. 51). As indicated by SHRM, young people are more willing to work for themselves as contractors, consultants, freelancers, and "taskers" [30]. Employees from younger generations value passion, purpose, flexibility, transparency, collaboration, trust, and autonomy [31]. Similarly, the survey of 18,000 professionals and students across these three generations from 19 countries conducted by INSEAD found that Gen Z favoured working for an international company, while Gen Y and Gen X professionals preferred starting their own business. However, these intentions differ between countries. Moreover, Gen Z was most enthusiastic about technologies and the potential of virtual reality [32].

Viewing work values from the perspective of Super (1980) as a relationship or material condition that one seeks to attain at the workplace, technologies seem to be an important condition for younger employees and, therefore, might represent an important workplace-related value which is not represented in MIQ. Similarly, such workplace aspects as global reach, entrepreneurial spirit, and excitement could provide new interesting insights.

4.3 Research methodology

4.3.1 Survey

We developed the questionnaire for measuring motivating factors and work values consisting of three sections:

1. Section 1 aimed to identify primary word associations related to the dream job. Respondents were asked to think about their ideal job and name three most important associations which come to their mind (these may be related to the job content, organisation, yourself, or similar).
2. Section 2 was devoted to workplace values. It includes 28 items which were based on original MIQ and WIP-C 21 items, adding four items about technologies, two items about global focus, and one about entrepreneurial orientation (21 + 7 items). The questionnaire consists of 28 items measuring work-related needs and values (see Table 4.4.1—items in italic are original and created for this research). Respondents were asked to rate the importance of these facet values on a 5-point scale from "unimportant" to "very important".
3. Section 3 was measuring the importance of workplace motivators and includes 20 items. First ten items are attributed to financial motivators, whereas the other ten items were measuring non-financial motivators.
4. Section 4 included items related to workplace well-being (hygge factors).
5. Final section measured demographic characteristics of the respondent. Age was measured using a five-year interval scale in 14 intervals starting from "before 31.12.1944" to "2000–2004" and "after 01.01.2005". For analysis, age was recorded and generation variables created using the following division of birth years: 1946–1964 Baby Boomers; 1965–1978 Generation X; 1977–1994 Generation Y; 1995–2004 Generation Z. Respondents were also asked to indicate their gender, education, employment experience, and nationality.

4.3.2 Research context

We have selected three countries for research: Latvia, Poland, and Portugal due to the simultaneous partial cultural heterogeneity of countries and partial economic homogeneity caused by a similar level of economic development within Europe. Latvia and Poland have a moderate level of innovation (moderate investors), while Portugal is on the borderline but already classifies as a strong innovator [33]. All countries have similar quality of human capital (below the EU average) among the European Union countries, according to the European Commission report [33]. Poland, Portugal, and Latvia also have similar values of the country's Global Competitiveness Index, which is presented in the report of the World Economic Forum. This report covers an analysis of 137 countries. Poland is in the 37th position in the ranking, and its Global Competitiveness overall score is 68.9; Portugal in the 34th place has reached 70.4 score, and Latvia—67 overall score, which places it in the 41st position [34]. Still, selected countries represent different parts of the EU from Southern to Eastern Europe.

In total, 1199 responses were collected; however, only two belonged to the Traditionalist generation, and the other two indicated nationality as "other", so the final sample retained for analysis is 1195 respondents. As recommended by [35], a sample size above 1000 is excellent for graded scale development. Respondents represent the three selected European countries: Latvia (n=729), Poland (n=208), and Portugal (n=258). Our sample consists of four generations: Baby Boomers (3.7%), Generation X (17.2%), millennials (35.5%), and Generation Z (43.7%). The gender distribution of the sample is 55.2% female; 44.6% male; and 0.2% chose not to indicate their gender. Sample demographics are presented in Table 4.2.

4.4 Results and discussion

Data were analysed in three stages—first two stages were related to the workplace values, while the third stage was related to work motivation and well-being.

First, exploratory factor analysis was performed to identify factors (overarching value) relevant in the contemporary workplace, and reliability analysis of the scales was performed. Secondly, the categorical regression analysis was performed to identify how the values are impacted by demographic variables. This allowed to identify if and how Generation Z work-related values are different.

The third part of analysis looked at differences between generation in respect to material and non-material motivators and well-being or hygge factors.

4.4.1 Stage one: identification of overarching values

For the first stage of the analysis (identification of overarching values), we use exploratory factor analysis (EFA) with oblique rotation, because it allows a degree of correlation between the factors ([36] p. 793). We choose

Table 4.2 Sample characteristics.

	Generation				Gender			Education				Total
	Gen Z	Gen Y	Gen X	Gen BB	Male	Female	Other	Basic	High school	Bachelor's degree	Master's degree	
Poland	192	11	5	0	89	117	2	0	202	6	0	208
Portugal	137	69	50	2	124	134	0	10	104	95	49	258
Latvia	193	344	150	42	319	410	0	89	121	266	253	729
Total	522	424	205	44	532	659	2	99	426	367	302	1195

Table 4.3 Vocational needs and value groups: summary of exploratory factor analysis (N=1195). (*Items in italic are original for this research.*)

Item number as in MIQ (new items in italic)	Item wording: On my ideal job, it is important that	Need/value (according to MIQ and new)	Rotated Loadings	Factor	Overarching Values and their meaning (EFA result for European sample)
26	the job would have a global focus	Global focus	.809		**Excitement and global focus—** conditions that ensure exciting, entrepreneurial, and globally focused environment, Cronbah's Alpha .797
27	I could work with colleagues from different cultures	Global citizenship	.784		
28	I can start my own business	Entrepreneurial spirit	.689		
19	I could do something different every day	Variety	.497		
5	I could give directions and instructions to others	Authority	.495		
22	I could do something exciting every day	Excitement	.447		
14	the job would provide for steady employment	Security	.710		**Comfort—**the condition that provides a stable and predictable, therefore stress-free, environment ensuring an individual's recognition and prestige, Cronbah's Alpha .765
6	I would be treated fairly by the company	Company policies and practices	.588		
12	I could receive recognition for the work I do	Recognition	.538		
20	the job would have good working conditions	Working conditions	.533		
7	my pay would compare well with that of other workers	Compensation	.495		
8	my co-workers would be easy to get along with	Co-workers	.494		

(*Continued*)

Item number as in MIQ (new items in italic)	Item wording: On my ideal job, it is important that	Need/value (according to MIQ and new)	Rotated Loadings	Factor	Overarching Values and their meaning (EFA result for European sample)
1	I make use of my abilities	Ability utilisation	.883		**Achievement**—conditions that encourage accomplishment and progress, Cronbah's Alpha .718
2	the work could give me a feeling of accomplishment	Achievement	.596		
4	the job would provide an opportunity for advancement	Advancement	.469		
9	I could try out my own ideas	Creativity	.375		
3	I could be busy all the time	Activity	.317		
17	I have supervisors who would back up their workers with management	Supervision— human relations	.844		**Supervision**—conditions that provide support for supervisors, Cronbah's Alpha .770
18	I would have supervisors who train workers well	Supervision— technical	.780		
24	I could use modern IT (e.g., cloud computing; video conferencing)	Technologies	.981		**Technologies**—conditions that provide a technology-enabled workplace, Cronbah's Alpha .786
23	I could work with new technologies	Technologies	.454		
25	I could work with artificial intelligence	Technologies (AI)	.404		
10	I could work alone	Independence	.553		**Independence**—conditions that increase personal control and initiative while maintaining honesty and strong moral principles, Cronbah's Alpha .534
21	I could plan my work with little supervision	Autonomy	.511		
11	I would never be pressured to do things that go against my sense of right and wrong	Moral values/ Integrity	.464		
13	I could make decisions on my own	Responsibility	.386		

(*Continued*)

Table 4.3 (Continued)

Item number as in MIQ (new items in italic)	Item wording: On my ideal job, it is important that	Need/value (according to MIQ and new)	Rotated Loadings	Factor	Overarching Values and their meaning (EFA result for European sample)
15	I could do things for other people	Social service	.604		**Altruism**— conditions that foster harmony and service to others, Cronbah's Alpha .582
16	I would be looked up to by others in my company and my community	Social status	.462		

promax rotation since it might be expected that certain values correlate as they are workplace related.

We obtained KMO statistic 0.89 (p=0.0005) which is well above the minimum criterion 0.5, indicating that the sample size is adequate for factor analysis. Seven factors with eigenvalues greater than one (Kaiser's criterion) were obtained in combination explaining 45.6% of the variance [36].

Table 4.4.1 shows the factor loadings after rotation. The obtained factor loadings range between 0.318 (v3) to 0.976 (v24). Factor loadings depend on sample size, and, according to ([36] p. 794), for samples > 1000 the loading should be greater than 0.162. All factor loadings were above 0.3, thus well above this threshold.

Cronbach's alpha coefficients range between 0.54 for independence and 0.58 for altruism to 0.79 for technologies and 0.8 for excitement, thus indicate acceptable internal consistency reliability. Two lower Cronbach's alphas are related to values measured by two items only what might explain lower values. Still, according to [37], sacrificing diversity of items to increase alpha hinders content validity, and since these items are original MIQ and correctly representing the value, they are retained. Further, we examined the meaning of the items and their overarching value and, based on TWA, provided explanations of the obtained overarching values.

Discriminant validity of identified seven overarching values is proved (see Table 4.4) since all the correlation coefficients between variables' pairs range between 0.190 and 0.599, thus are below 0.7. Thus, multicollinearity is not a problem, and the factors measure different variables and should not be grouped.

Results of exploratory factor analyses (EFA) show a slightly different value structure for the European sample than it was in MIQ and WIP-C studies. We identified seven value groups (see Table 4.4.1) which are discussed below. Thus, six MIQ overarching values in the current European sample

Table 4.4 Descriptive statistics and correlations (n=1195).

	MEAN	STEDEV	1	2	3	4	5	6	7	8	9	10
Gender	1.56	0.5	1									
Birth year	10.4	2.3	-.021	1								
Education	2.74	0.95	-.050	-.627**	1							
Employment	1.44	0.64	.062*	.498**	-.527**	1						
Achievement	4.15	0.57	.007	-.028	.120**	-.087**	1					
Supervision	4.25	0.78	.073*	-.021	.106**	-.111	.437**	1				
Comfort	4.34	0.57	.072*	-.015	.110**	-.137**	.565**	.550**	1			
Altruism	3.88	0.79	.036	-.055	.115**	-.092**	.438**	.442**	.464**	1		
Independence	3.77	0.64	.048	-.063*	.104**	-.056	.282**	.258**	.317**	.264**	1	
Excitement	3.35	0.8	-.017	.211**	-.165**	.178**	.468**	.278**	.319**	.373**	.266**	1
Technologies	3.4	0.9	-.082**	.093**	-.046	.133**	.291**	.114**	.197**	.190**	.191**	.599**

**. Correlation is significant at the 0.01 level (two-tailed).

*. Correlation is significant at the 0.05 level (two-tailed).

scored as four values: comfort, achievement, altruism, and independence. Two new values we label excitement and global focus and technologies.

- Factor one: excitement and global focus. The factor which explains the highest percentage of the variance appeared to be related to the new focal values—global focus and citizenship, entrepreneurial spirit, and excitement. Two MIC values (authority and variety) also loaded on factor number one. We label this value "excitement and global focus," meaning "conditions that ensure an exciting, entrepreneurial, and globally-focused environment". We argue that the original MIQ value variety (statement "I could do something different every day"), in current understanding, could mean an exciting work environment, which is not boring and repetitive.
- Factor two: comfort. The current study grouped three values according to TWA (comfort, safety, and status) in one overarching value group consisting of six facet values. We name the value "comfort," meaning the condition that provides stable and predictable, therefore stress-free, environment, ensuring an individual's recognition and prestige.
- Factor three: achievement. Overarching value "achievement" appeared to include five facet values including creativity. We argue that the statement "I could try out my own ideas," in line with other statements, appears to be related to personal achievement, and the meaning of the value remains the same as according to TWA.
- Factor four: supervision. Supervision-related values in MIQ are placed under overarching value "safety". However, for the European sample, they loaded as a separate factor. We label this value "supervision" and define it as a condition that provides support from supervisors.
- Factor five: independence. We label the next overarching value group identified in this study "independence," meaning conditions that increase personal control and initiative while maintaining honesty and strong moral principles. This value includes four values: independence, integrity, autonomy, and responsibility. We argue that all segments related to these facet values better characterise the condition in which the individual can be independent in the workplace.
- Factor six: altruism. Value "altruism" appears to contain only two items since "moral values" (as in MIQ) are loaded on the independence factor. The remaining two items perfectly characterise conditions that foster harmony and service to others, which define altruism. We argue that MIQ value "social status" is related to harmony and "social service" to service to others.
- Factor seven: technologies. The final factor includes three statements, and all of them are related to various levels of advanced technologies in the workplace. We label this value "technologies" and define it as conditions that provide a technology-enabled workplace.

Comparing values, as rated by all respondents, comfort (M=4.34; SD=.57), supervisory support (M=4.25; SD=.78), and achievement (M=4.15; SD=.57) showed the highest scores, followed by altruism (M=3.88; SD=.79) and independence (M=3.77; SD=.64). Excitement (M=3.35; SD=.80) and technologies (M=3.4; SD=.90) are scored lower. Friedman test chi-square value 2248.8*** indicates that differences between value scores are statistically significant.

Thus, the fundamental values important for individuals in the contemporary workplace appear to be similar as indicated by MIQ—comfort, which includes MIQ values safety—conditions that establish predictability and stability; and status—conditions that provide recognition and prestige; and supervision, which scores in MIQ as under safety value, as well as achievement, which now includes, in addition to original MIQ focal values, also activity and advancement.

4.4.2 Stage two: predicting work value score from the country, gender, employment, and age

The final part of analysis aimed to determine if work values are significantly predicted by country, gender, employment, and age. Categorical regression analysis was performed using dummy variables created for countries, gender (excluding respondents who did not indicate their gender), employment, and age group (with five-year intervals) as independent variables, and seven work-related values as dependent variables. Following [2], optimal scaling was used to the categorical data age group to be used. The lowest value was assigned to age group 1944–1949; therefore, positive beta weights are indicative of increased importance of value by younger respondents, while negative beta indicates a decrease in importance by younger respondents. Dummy variables for Poland and Portugal were created using Latvia as the baseline.

For gender, positive betas are indicative of the increased importance of value by females. For work experience, negative betas are indicative of a decrease in importance by not employed respondents. Since two respondents choose not to indicate their gender, they were excluded from regression analysis, and the retained sample size was 1193. This analysis allowed to evaluate and compare the strengths of impact on work values from the country, gender, employment, and age groups. A summary of the results is provided in Table 4.5.

Categorical regressions showed that country significantly predicts all work values. Portugal scored higher for achievement (mean values Port = 4.37; Pol = 4.09; Latv = 4.08), comfort (mean values Port = 4.54; Pol = 4.21; Latv = 4.32), altruism (mean values Port = 4.17; Pol = 3.75; Latv=3.82), excitement (mean values Port = 3.89; Pol = 3.75; Latv = 3.18) and technologies (only than Latvia), but lower for independence (mean 3.46). Poland scored higher for independence (mean values Pol = 3.98; Port = 3.46; Latv = 3.82), and higher than Latvia for excitement and technologies. Representation of country affects all work-related values.

Table 4.5 Predicting work value score by country, gender, employment, and age: categorical regression results (N=1193).

Overarching Values	R-Squared	F	Country		Gender	Education	Work experience	Age
			β (Poland)	β (Portugal)	β	β	β	β
Achievement	0.068	14.51***	0.13*	0.32***	0.03	0.09***	−0.07*	0.02
Supervision	0.048	9.87***	−0.27*	0.09	0.14**	0.09**	−0.07	0.04**
Comfort	0.071	15.04***	−0.01	0.25***	0.11***	0.07**	−0.12***	0.03**
Altruism	0.055	11.51***	0.05	0.38***	0.08	0.096**	−0.08**	0.01
Independence	0.1	21.86***	0.21***	−0.32***	0.06	0.09***	−0.08***	0.00
Excitement	0.22	56.23***	0.55***	0.80***	−0.01	−0.01	0	0.03**
Technologies	0.11	22.62***	0.56***	0.57***	−0.14**	0.07*	0.08	0.01

*** . significant at the 0.001 level.
** . significant at the 0.01 level.
* . significant at the 0.05 level.

Gender significantly predicts supervision, comfort, and technologies. Supervision and comfort values are more important for females, whereas working with technologies appears to be more important for males.

Our results show that the level of education does impact an individual's vocational needs. Respondents with higher education (bachelor or master's degrees) tend to score higher on achievement, supervision, comfort, altruism, and independence if compared to those still studying. Although young adults have developed enough maturity to have a sense of their anticipated future biographies, their experiences are still formative in that transitions from formal education to work/careers may be ongoing [38].

Work experience significantly predicts achievement, comfort, altruism, and independence values—these values are less important for non-working respondents.

Age groups appear to be significant predictors only for three work-related values—supervision, comfort, and excitement. Positive beta coefficients indicate that these values are more important for younger respondents. However, some authors suggest that differences between generations are more context than age-dependent [39].

The final analysis aimed to evaluate the strength of predicting value scored from generational groups. Generation Z was assigned the lowest value and Baby Boomers the highest; therefore, positive beta weights are indicative of the increased importance of value by older generations, and negative beta weights are indicative of the increased importance of value by younger generations. Categorical regression results are presented in Table 4.6.

Categorical regressions suggested that generation have no impact on achievement, supervision, comfort, and altruism. These findings are in line with [28] who found no generational differences for altruistic values.

Categorical regressions suggested that generation significantly predicted three overarching values: independence, excitement, and technologies. Independence appears to be less important for Gen Z (M=3.71), but most important for Gen Y (M=3.81), Gen X, and Gen BB, scoring in the middle (M=3.8). Excitement is significantly more important for Gen Z (M=3.58) and less important for Gen BB (M=2.92). Similarly, technologies appear to be more important for Gen Z (M=3.53) than for other generations (M=3.3).

Our results show that the work-related values of four studied generations are not so different. Similarly, surveying Chinese people, Yi and colleagues did not find extensive differences [40]. Only three out of seven values are impacted by generation—independence is more important for older generations, while excitement and technologies are more important for younger generations. As found by [41], millennials have grown up during the Information Age. They connected to each other and use technology for work, fun, or when the information was needed, thus they value technologies. We

Table 4.6 Predicting work value score by country, gender, employment, and age: categorical regression results (N=1193).

Overarching Values	R-Squared	F	Country		Gender	Education	Work experience	Age
			β (Poland)	β (Portugal)	β	β	β	β
Achievement	0.068	14.51***	0.13*	0.32***	0.03	0.09***	−0.07*	0.02
Supervision	0.048	9.87***	−0.27*	0.09	0.14**	0.09**	−0.07	0.04**
Comfort	0.071	15.04***	−0.01	0.25***	0.11***	0.07**	−0.12***	0.03**
Altruism	0.055	11.51***	0.05	0.38***	0.08	0.096**	−0.08**	0.01
Independence	0.1	21.86***	0.21***	−0.32***	0.06	0.09***	−0.08***	0.00
Excitement	0.22	56.23***	0.55***	0.80***	−0.01	−0.01	0	0.03**
Technologies	0.11	22.62***	0.56***	0.57***	−0.14**	0.07*	0.08	0.01

*** . significant at the 0.001 level.
** . significant at the 0.01 level.
* . significant at the 0.05 level.

found technology to be more important for Generation Z. Similarly, analysing the work-related values of Generation Z in Poland, workplace behaviour of Generation Z employees is radically different from that of older generations' [12]. See Figure 4.1.

As concluded by Campbell and colleagues, in spite of the usefulness of the generational construct, "generational differences exist, and grouping people into generations is useful even though the differences tend to build over birth years" [24].

4.4.3 Stage three: importance of motivating factors and well-being

In the third stage of the analysis, we deal with the importance of motivating factors and well-being. The Table 4.7 shows descriptive statistics of the variables and Spearman correlations for full sample.

Looking at all respondents together, it is evident that material motivation prevails over non-material (paired sample t-test t=13.67***); however, well-being factors are stated to be even more important (paired sample t=19.48***).

Differences between countries were analysed using one-way ANOVA test (see Figure 4.2), and results indicated statistically significant differences between hygge factors and material motivators for all countries, but for non-material motivators, differences between Poland and Portugal appeared to be nonsignificant.

Looking at differences between generations (see Figure 4.3), it is evident that Gen Z put more value at material and non-material motivators than other generations. Interestingly, that well-being factors appear to be not so important for them—differences between generations are non-significant (ANOVA test F=.93).

Looking in detail at material motivators (see Figure 4.4), it is evident that Gen Z care about educational bonuses (M5); healthy lifestyle benefits (M7); childcare benefits (M8); additional benefits, for example, insurance (M9) and also retirement benefits (M10); however, this factor is more important for Baby Boomers. The differences are presented in Figure 4.4 below.

However, since Gen Z respondents are mostly without employment experience, it can be assumed that presence or absence of work experience can also cause differences in the importance put on motivating factors. Indeed, independent sample t-test (see Figure 4.5) indicated statistically significant differences for material (t=−4.08***) and non-material motivators (t=−6.41***).

Looking at non-material motivators (see Figure 4.5) in detail, Generation Z appear to be significantly different in respect to work security (M11)—it is very important for them to have permanent work contract. They will prefer to work in public sector organisation. They would highly value working in a socially responsible company—one which engages in local matters,

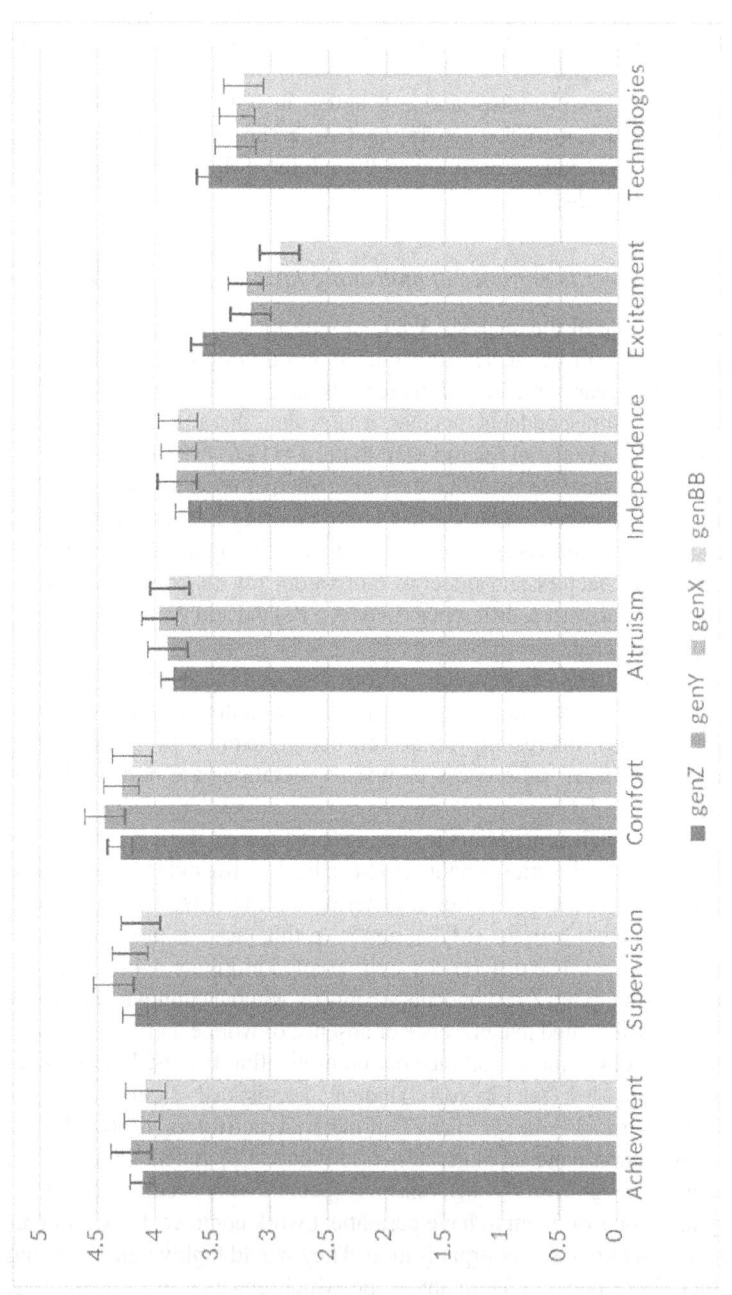

Figure 4.1 Importance of work values by generations.

Table 4.7 Descriptive statistics and correlations for motivating factors.

Factor	No.	No. of indicators	Cronbach's alpha	Mean*	Standard deviation	1	2
Material motivators	1	10	.85	3.95	.64		
Non-material motivators	2	7	.63	3.72	.62	.56**	
Well-being (hygge) factors	3	8	.81	4.07	.58	.52**	.48**

* in five-point Likert scale, where 1—unimportant; 5—very important

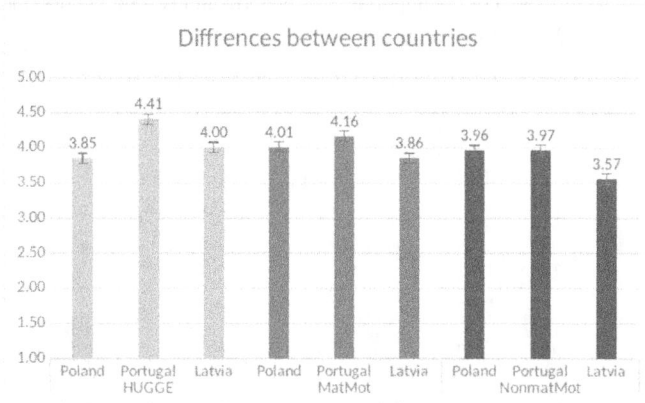

Figure 4.2 Comparison of the importance of motivating factors across countries.

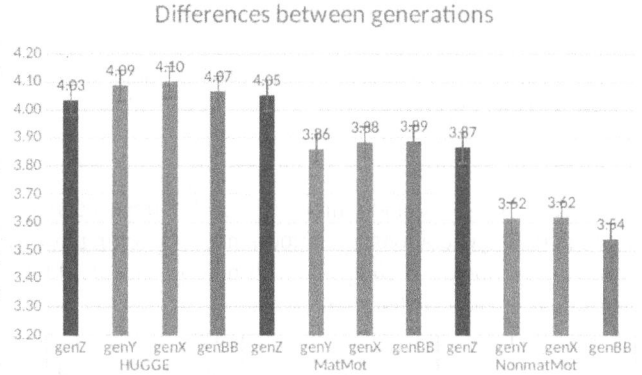

Figure 4.3 Comparison of the importance of motivating factors across generations.

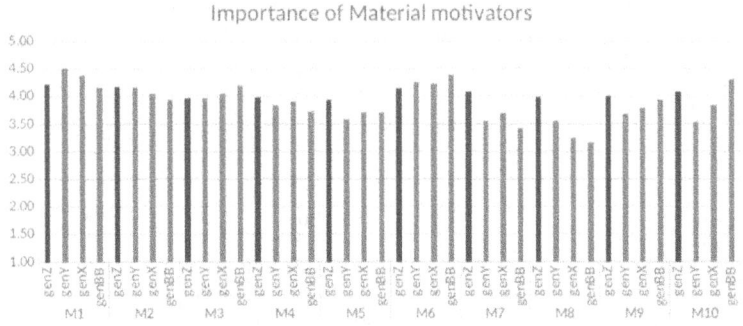

Figure 4.4 Comparison of the importance of material motivating factors (indicator level) across generations.

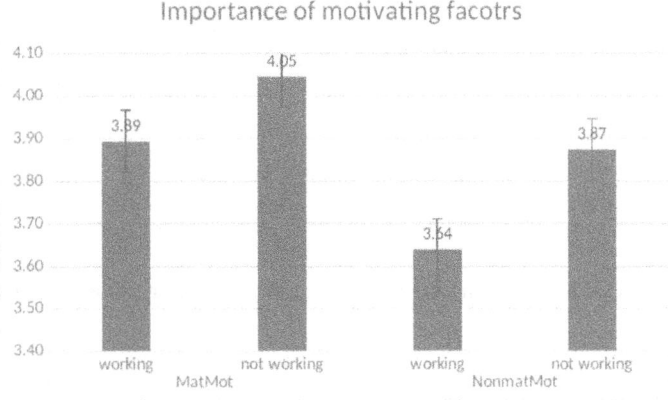

Figure 4.5 Importance of material and non-material motivators for working and non-working respondents.

social and ecological issues, and which aids local entrepreneurship. They also, more than other generations, put importance on working in a dynamically developing business—a company with high profit rate, high profitability, increasing its market share.

Table 4.8 shows the breakdown of the importance of all eight well-being (hygge) factors as indicated by respondents from different generations. Only four indicators out of eight show statistically significant differences—they are indicated in bold.

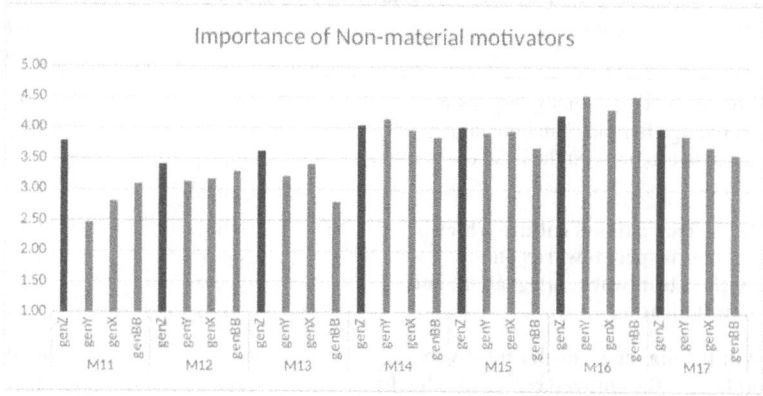

Figure 4.6 Comparison of the importance of non-material motivating factors (indicator level) across generations.

Table 4.8 Vocational needs and value groups: summary of exploratory factor analysis (N=1195).

Well-being indicator	Generation	Mean value
W1: keeping balance between your private and professional life	Gen Z	4.28
	Gen Y	4.51
	Gen X	4.49
	Gen BB	4.18
W2: possibility of choosing my own benefits from a list offered by the employer	**Gen Z**	**3.95**
	Gen Y	3.74
	Gen X	3.88
	Gen BB	3.73
W3: wages are adjusted to the employee's competencies and results	Gen Z	4.15
	Gen Y	4.17
	Gen X	4.18
	Gen BB	4.16
W4: cosy and interestingly designed office space with plants and eco-friendly elements	Gen Z	3.77
	Gen Y	3.63
	Gen X	3.69
	Gen BB	3.96
	Total	3.71
W5: flat organisational structure, egalitarianism, and transparency at workplace	Gen Z	3.77
	Gen Y	3.93
	Gen X	3.90
	Gen BB	3.89

(Continued)

Table 4.8 (Continued)

Well-being indicator	Generation	Mean value
W6: employer is socially responsible (including "fair play" and not taking aggressive actions on the business market)	Gen Z	3.94
	Gen Y	3.83
	Gen X	3.93
	Gen BB	3.93
W7: organisational culture which includes respect towards one another, teamwork, integration, and communication	Gen Z	4.22
	Gen Y	4.45
	Gen X	4.35
	Gen BB	4.39
W8: the manager/ leader positively motivates the employees, is available to everyone, and is part of the team	Gen Z	4.20
	Gen Y	4.44
	Gen X	4.38
	Gen BB	4.33

Interestingly, Generation Y appears to be different—indicating factors W1, W7, and W8 as more important than other generations. However, the factor which appears to be significantly more important for Generation Z is W2: possibility of choosing my own benefits from a list offered by the employer.

The results from the quantitative data analysis are supported by analysis of qualitative data—the results form survey Section 1—word associations. Figure 4.7 presents the word cloud which was generated for Gen Z respondents' primary associations which they indicated for an "ideal job".

Not surprisingly, "salary" appears as the most frequently mentioned word. This supports the results presented in Figure 4.3 indicating that Gen Z put more importance on material motivators than other generations do. Interestingly, the second frequent word is "team"; however, data in Table 4.8 indicate that Gen Z scored indicator W7: organisational culture which includes respect towards one another, teamwork, integration, and communication lower than other generations. Obviously, work teams and colleagues are important for all generations, and Gen Z is not exception here. The following examples can be mentioned as Gen Z associations with an ideal job:

"An approachable team focused on achieving a common goal";
"Understanding attitude from management";

Other important motivating aspect which frequently appeared in the associations is "free" and "schedule". Gen Z mentioned *"informal environment"* and *"flexible work schedule" as associations with an ideal job.*

Figure 4.7 Comparison of the importance of non-material motivating factors (indicator level) across generations.

Source: Created with: https://wordart.com/.

Content analysis of association with ideal job for Generation Z respondents revealed associations related to excitement-related work values (see results presented in Figure 4.1). This value represents conditions that ensure an exciting, entrepreneurial, and globally focused environment. The following questions are good illustrations of the above:

"I don't consider it a job, but a hobby";
"There is no feeling that I am wasting my time";
"It's a pleasure to go to work";
"The work should bring joy and a sense of satisfaction";
"A hobby that still pays a salary";
"Interesting; corresponding to my interests".
"Meaningful and valuable (both in my and society's perception)";
"To find moral fulfilment";
"Created your own business, company"

Surprisingly, technology-related statements appeared rarely in the list. We explain this result to the notion that Generation Z cannot imagine life and workplace without technologies; therefore, they assume the presence of technologies as evident [29].

4.5 Conclusions

Results of the present empirical research suggest work-related values in 21st century Europe are similar to those identified by Minnesota Importance Questionnaire (MIQ) and WIP-C instruments; however, the instruments for measuring work values should be updated. We tested the Minnesota Importance Questionnaire in European countries and propose additional vocational needs and alternative grouping of vocational values and inclusion of technologies and excitement-related values. The analysis showed that the seven-dimension content is clear, and with no content overlap, it could be considered as an improvement on existing work values scales.

Our results show that Generation Z is different in the following workplace-related aspects:

1. Gen Z work values are similar to other generations; however, they differ in respect to such values as *excitement and global focus* and *technologies*—for Gen Z, it is important that work is exciting and to have a technologically enhanced workplace.
2. For Gen Z the following material motivators are more important: *educational bonuses, healthy lifestyle benefits, childcare, insurance benefits*, and they also care about social guarantees.
3. Out of non-material motivators, Gen Z value *work security*. They expect from their *employer to be socially responsible and a dynamically developing company*.
4. For Gen Z the importance of well-being factors is like for other generations; however, more than other generations, they put importance on *possibility of choosing my own benefits from a list offered by the employer*.

Bibliography

[1] Barley S.R., Bechky B.A., Milliken F.J. (2017), *The Changing Nature of Work: Careers, Identities, and Work Lives in the 21st Century*, Academy of Management Discoveries, 3, pp. 111–115.

[2] Hansen J.I.C., Leuty M.E. (2012), *Work values across generations*, Journal of Career Assessment, 20, 34–52.

[3] *Deloitte. Deloitte Human Capital trends* [Tiessaiste] (2017). https://www2.deloitte.com/content/dam/Deloitte/global/Documents/ HumanCapital/hc-2017-global-human-capital-trends-gx.pdf (accessed: 7.11.2019).

[4] Maurer, R. (2017), *What Do Young Job Seekers Expect to Earn Around the World?* [Tiessaiste]. www.shrm.org/resourcesandtools/hr-topics/ talent-acquisition/pages/young-job-seekers-expect-earn-around-world.aspx (accessed: 13.01.2019).

[5] Milligan S. (2014), *SHRM HR Magazine* [Tiessaiste], 26 November. www.hrmagazine-digital.com/hrmagazine/november_2014?search_term=millennials%20born&doc_id=-1&pg=26#pg26 (accessed: 04.11.2016).

[6] Roepe R.L. (2017), *SHRM HR Magazine* [Tiessaiste], 46, April. www.hrma-gazine-digital.com/hrmagazine/april_2017?search_term= millennials%20 born&doc_id=-1&pg=46#pg46 (accessed: 29.04.2017).

[7] Ebner K. (2018), *Validation of the German career decision-making profile: An updated 12-factor version*, Journal of Career Assessment, 26, 111–136.

[8] Konrad A. (2000), *Sex differences and similarities in job attribute preferences: A meta-analysis*, Psychological Bulletin, 126, 539–641.

[9] Gilbert R.G., Sohi R.S., McEachern A.G. (2008), *Measuring work preferences: A multidimensional tool to enhance career self-management*, Career Development International, 13, 56–78.

[10] Baruch Y., Rousseau D.M. (2019), *Integrating psychological contracts and ecosystems in career studies and management*, Academy of Management Annals, 13, 84–111.

[11] McCloy R. (1999), *Development of the O*NET™ Computerized Work Importance Profiler*, NC: National Center for O*NET Development.

[12] Lazanyi K., Bilan Y. (2017), *Generation Z on the labour market: Do they trust others within their workplace?*, Polish Journal of Management Studies, 16, 78–93.

[13] Ukleja, M., Espinoza C. (2016), *Managing the Millennials*, 2nd edition, NJ: John Wiley & Sons.

[14] Bourne B.B. (2019), *Phenomenological study of response to organisational change: Baby boomers, generation X, and generation Y*, bez viet.: University of Phoenix, ProQuest Dissertations.

[15] Twenge J.M., Campbell S.M. (2008), *Generational differences in psychological traits and their impact on the workplace*, Journal of Managerial Psychology, 23, 862–877.

[16] Dawis R.W., Lofquist L.H., Weiss D.J. (1968), *A theory of work adjustment*, Minnesota Studies in Vocational Rehabilitation, Minneapolis: University of Minnesota Press.

[17] Librizzi U.A., Dahling J.J. (2014), *Integrating the theory of work adjustment and attachment theory to predict job turnover intentions*, Journal of Career Development, 1–19.

[18] Super D.E. (1980), *A life-span, life-space approach to career development*, Journal of Occupational Psychology, 52, 129–148.

[19] Dawes R.V., Lofquist L.H. (1984), *A Psychological Theory of Work Adjustment*, Minneapolis: University of Minnesota Press.

[20] Dawis R.V. (2005), *The Minnesota Theory of Work Adjustment*, in *Career Development and Counseling: Putting Theory and Research to Work*, ed. Brown S.D., Lent R.W., Hoboken, NJ: John Wiley, pp. 3–23.

[21] Schein E.H. (1996), *Career Anchors Revisited: Implications for Career Development in the 21st Century*, Academy of Management Executive, pp. 80–88.

[22] Gay E.G. (1971), *Manual for the Minnesota Importance Questionnaire*, Minnesota: Studies in Vovational Rehabilitation, 28.

[23] Jaeger H. (1985), *Generations in history: Reflections on a controversial concept*, History and Theory, 24, 273–292.

[24] Campbell S.M., Twenge J.M., Campbell K.W. (2017), *Fuzzy but useful constructs: Making sense of the differences between generations*, Work, Aging and Retirement, 3, 130–139.

[25] Johnson, M., Johnson L. (2010), *Generations, Inc.: From Boomers to Link-sters—Managing the Friction Between Generations at Work*, New York: AMACOM.

[26] Crumpacker M., Crumpacker J.M. (2007), *Succession planning and generational stereotypes: Should HR consider age-based values and attitudes a relevant factor or a passing fad?*, Public Personnel Management, 36, 349–369.

[27] Keldsen D., Koulopoulus T. (2014), *The Gen Z Effect: The Six Forces Shaping the Future of Business*, Brookline: Bibliomotion.

[28] Twenge J.M. (2010), *Generational difference in work values: Leisure and extrinsic values increasing, social and intrinsic values decreasing*, Journal of Management, 36, 1117–1142.

[29] Ahmed Z. (2015), *The impact of emerging technologies on human values*, International Journal of Core Engineering & Management, 1, 11–58.

[30] Gayeski D. (2015), *Will Generation Z Even Care about HR Technology?* [Tiessaiste] 6 July. www.shrm.org/resourcesandtools/hr-topics/ technology/pages/will-generation-z-even-care-about-hr-technology.aspx (accessed: 03.12.2020).

[31] Bond S. (2016), *The new rules of engagement*, International Journal of Market Research, 58, 351–353.

[32] Rao V.D., Bresman H. (2017), *A survey of 19 countries shows how generations X, Y, and Z are—and aren't—different*, Harvard Business Review, 25 August.

[33] European Commission. (2018), *European Innovation Scoreboard 2018*, Luxembourg: Publication Office of the European Union.

[34] World Economic Forum. (2019), *The Global Competitiveness Report 2019*, Geneva: World Economic Forum.

[35] Comrey A., Lee H. (1992), *A First Course in Factor Analysis*, NJ: Lawrence Erlbaum Associates, Inc New York.

[36] Field A. (2018), *Discovering Statistics Using IBM SPSS Statistics*, 5th edition, bez viet.: SAGE.

[37] Eunseong C., Seonghoon K. (2014), *Cronbach's coefficient alpha: Well known but poorly understood*, Organisational Research Methods, 1–24.

[38] McDonald P.K. (2018), *How 'flexible' are careers in the anticipated life course of young people?*, Human Relations, 71, 23–46.

[39] Deal J.J. (2007), *Retiring the generation gap: How employees young and old find common grounds*, San Francisco: Jossey-Bass.

[40] Yi X., Ribbens B., Morgan C.N. (2010), *Generational differences in China: Career implications*, Career Development International, 15, 601–620.

[41] Mitkova L., Mariak V. (2015), *The first globalized generation—generation Y*, 15th International Scientific Conference Globalization and Its Socio-Economic Consequences, University of Zilina, Zilina.

[42] Ryan T. (2017), *The Next Generation*, NJ: John Wiley & Sons.

[43] North M.S. (2019), *A GATE to understanding 'older' workers: Generation, age, tenure, experience*, Academy of Management Annals, 13, 414–443.

[44] Lester S.W. (2012), *Actual versus perceived generational differences at work*, Journal of Leadership & Organizational Studies, 19, 341–354.
[45] Jurkiewicz C.L. (2000), *Generation X and the public employee*, Public Personnel Management, 29, 55–74.

5 Current research methods in mathematical and computer modelling of motivation management

Agnieszka Niemczynowicz
and Radosław Antoni Kycia

In the last century, we can observe a dynamical development of techniques applied to analysis of data in the management. One of the most influential reasons is rapid development in the field of computer science, especially in machine learning (ML) and artificial intelligence (AI), and the significant socioeconomic changes, which place enormous demands on the improvement of management.

Researches on management have been receiving more and more attention for new, more effective methods and techniques in order to replace it with new ones which adjust conditions and assumptions to practical management knowledge. A popular mathematical method for understanding and modelling in theoretical and practical management usually comes from statistic and multivariate data analysis. Several papers indicated that besides classical statistical methods such as ANOVA [1], structural equations modelling [2, 3], polynomial regression [5], exploratory factor analysis [4], and the like were adopted for management data analysis. As often as not, data analysis mentioned methods is processing in SPSS or other statistical programs.

Recent, researches on analysing dataset directs to more sophisticated methods connecting with machine learning, i.e., used by a large number systems across various areas including social science, management, natural science, and any other research areas. Data structure for machine learning focuses on tasks such as classifications, prediction, clustering, and much more. For modelling with ML and AI, what's important is appropriate design pipeline and tools which are able to realise proposed methodology.

In the following paragraphs, we will illustrate and propose the pipeline and the modern data analysis methods for motivation management using power of Python programming language.

DOI: 10.4324/9781003353935-5

5.1 Introduction to Python programming

5.1.1 Overview of computer methods in data science

The beginning of the 21st century started with an unprecedented abundance of data of various types. The demand for new flexible tools for their analysis resulted in fast-developing areas of data analysis, including big data and machine learning.

There are various standard tools that are used in data analysis. Their use depend on the specific needs in the company/faculty and the level of mastering of technical details of computer programming. We present some authoritative lists of these tools below.

Commercial tools

* Microsoft products: Excel®[12] and Visual Basic scripting language for adding new functionality to the standard spreadsheet. It is a part of the Microsoft Office suite. There are also alternatives such as Open Source project, e.g., LibreOffice [13].
* Dell Software product: Statistica®[14] can be considered as a set of (from simple to very advanced) statistical tools that can be used for almost any problem met in statistics.
* SAS Institute product: SAS [15] which is also a Swiss knife for statistical analysis.

"Free" tools

* R language [16]—programming language aimed at statistical analysis and a big set of libraries for various statistical analysis.
* Python [17]—a general-purpose higher-level programming language with many programming libraries. Some of them are related to data analysis.
* Julia programming language and libraries [18]—new general-purpose programming language designed for fast numerical computations; however, currently there are not many native libraries for data analysis—libraries from other languages, like Python or R, can be used.

The term "free" means that, generally, they are open-source and free of charge; however, some libraries and components may be commercial or for a fee.

Commercial products are usually more user-friendly, designed with an easy-to-use graphical user interface. Above "free" tools are mainly programming languages with specialised libraries, and the use of these solutions heavily relies on programming skills of users.

In this chapter, we present a Python-oriented approach to the analysis of social data. We will back up our choice with the fact that, although at the beginning there is a small inconvenience in learning the basics of programming, this tool gives the user more flexibility and control in designing analysis tools. Another essential argument for selecting Python is the fact that it is also a general-purpose programming language with plenty of libraries for almost any task that computers can do. These libraries, if needed, can also be used in data analysis script.

In the next two paragraphs, we present tools that increase Python productivity in data analysis—proper setup of the programming environment and then focus on some basic and fast introduction to Python programming.

5.1.2 Setting up environment

Generally, Python can be installed on any operating system—Microsoft Windows, various flavors of Linux/Unix, and macOS. Technical details of Python installation can be found in, e.g., [6, 10].

The core of basic yet powerful data analysis in Python is the set of a few libraries:

- NumPy [19]—fast arrays/matrices and set of operations on them.
- SciPy [20]—set of various algorithms useful in science.
- Pandas [21]—basic library for data analysis. It includes DataFrames type that reminds a spreadsheet.
- Matplotlib [22]—powerful library for visualisation.
- Seaborn [23]—provide additional features for data visualisation to Matplotlib.
- Scikit-learn [24]—powerful library for machine learning.

Currently, there is version 2.x and 3.x of the language. Here x represents some additional numbering scheme. There are small differences between these versions. We will focus on the 3.x version since the version 2.x is currently not supported.

In Linux-like systems, all the tools mentioned in this section can be installed easily by a standard package manager. For Windows or macOS, the better approach is to use software distributions that include all necessary packages, e.g.,

- Anaconda [26]—for Windows, macOS, and Linux.
- Python(x, y) [27]—for Windows only.
- WinPython [28]—for Windows only.

The libraries, as mentioned above, are available under the standard Python interpreter/shell [17] or under a more user-friendly shell called IPython [25]. The work with such an interpreter is based on idea of REPL—read, evaluate, print, loop. It means that the shell waits for a command to input by the user. When the user writes it, then the command is evaluated, and the result is printed. Finally, the process repeats.

For standard Python interpreter, the command prompt is ">>>", and for IPython, the input and output is enumerated.

The simplest "Hello world" program in interpreter is:

```
print("Hello World")
```

The function print() prints its argument on screen. The argument of this function is the string (i.e., collection of characters): "Hello World"—it is indicated by surrounding quotation marks. In Python console, it looks as follows:

```
Python 3.5.2 (default, Nov 12 2018, 13:43:14)
[GCC 5.4.0 20160609] on linux
Type "help", "copyright", "credits" or "license" for more information.
>>> print("Hello World")
Hello World
>>>
```

The session can be terminated by quit() or by the standard combination Ctrl + D.

The same interaction in IPython console looks as follows:

```
Python 3.5.2 (default, Nov 12 2018, 13:43:14)
Type 'copyright', 'credits' or 'license' for more information
IPython 6.5.0 -- An enhanced Interactive Python. Type '?' for help.

In [1]: print("Hello World")
Hello World

In [2]:
```

We can quit by simply writing quit or Ctrl + D shortcut. One can observe that the input is enumerated. Besides, the arrows up and down can be used for recalling previous commands, and left, right arrows for editing input.

The code of Python can also be written in an unformatted text file with usual extension ".py". It can be loaded to the interpreter and executed line by line. The "Hello World" program saved in "HelloWorld.py" file looks like

```
#!/usr/bin/env python3  #you can change to python2

#this is one line comment

print("Hello World")
```

The first two letters (#!), called shebang, inform a Linux operating system that the file has to be interpreted in Python 3.x interpreter. Shebang must be at the top of the file to work properly. For other operating systems, it is a comment starting from "#" sign and ending with the end line. The code from Linux Bash shell can be run by executing:

```
python3 HelloWorld.py
```

One can also run it similarly to a normal program, first by setting execution rights in Bash shell:

```
chmod +x HelloWorld.py
```

and then start the script

```
./HelloWorld.py
```

Under IPython console, one can also run the script by "magic command" (that starts from %):

```
In [1]: %run HelloWorld.py
Hello World
```

A list of all magic commands for the IPython shell, which is useful, can be obtained by "%lsmagic".

Skills to use the console is essential; however, the more effective approach to write a Python code is to use advanced IDE (integrated development environment). One example designed for scientific computing is Spyder IDE [29]. An example window is presented in Figure 5.1.

One of the drawbacks of this approach is that the only place where additional information/description can be added are comments. It is a problem when, as it happens usually in data analysis, fragments of a Python code interwove with descriptions, equations, and plots. This issue is resolved by Jupyter Notebooks [30], which introduces the narrative code that can present the whole path of reasoning in a data analysis. The Jupyter Notebook can be used as a report from analysis. The notebook is an interface to Python (and other programming languages) that runs in a web browser. It is split into cells. Each cell can contain code, text, or raw text. Images and movies can also be embedded. The notebook can be structured using different levels of headings. An example of the Jupyter Notebook is presented in Figure 5.2. Notebooks can also be converted into Python code, PDF, and LaTeX files, and also to HTML webpages. These features make them ideal for data analysis.

Having known basic ideas behind installing and running simple Hello World script, in the next section, a quick introduction to Python programming language will be presented.

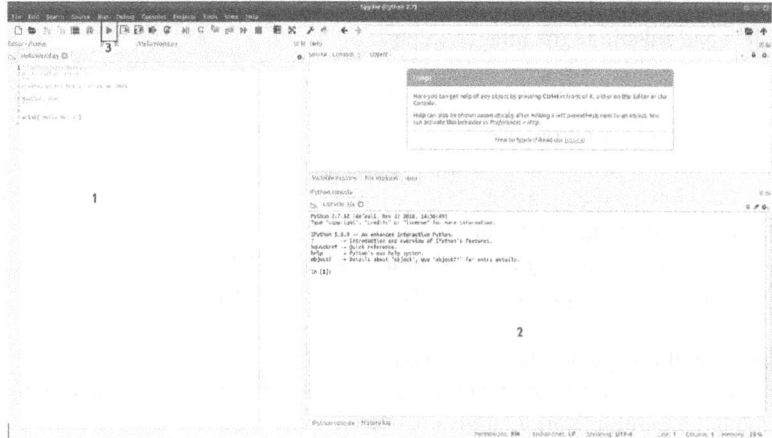

Figure 5.1 Window of Spyder IDE 3.3.8. The part one of the widow is an advanced Python editor. The part two is an IPython console where also the results of the script are displayed. The icon three can be used to run the script written in one.

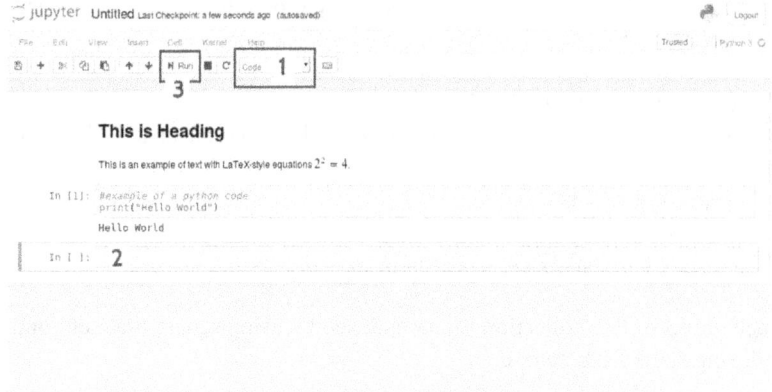

Figure 5.2 Jupyter Notebook that is running in a web browser. One presents a list where the type of active cell is setup. Two is an empty cell. Three is a run icon that evaluates current active cell—shortcut Shift + Enter does the same.

5.1.3 Elements of Python

This section contains an elementary introduction to Python programming. In-depth exposition can be found in [9, 11].

In Python, the variable is created at the moment it is used—this is an example of dynamically typed language. For example, we can create a variable a and substitute the integer value 2:

```
a=2
```

The examples of types are:

- Int—integers, e.g., a = 2.
- Float—floating point real values, e.g., a = 2.0.
- Char—character, e.g., a = "a" or a = 'a' or a = """ a""".
- Complex—complex numbers, e.g., a = 1 + j2, where .

The type of a variable can be checked by type(a).

Numerical data can be manipulated by arithmetic operations as addition, subtraction, multiplication, division, e.g.,

```
>>> a=2
>>> b=3
>>> a+b
5
>>> a+3
5
```

More complicated types can be created by grouping simple types using collections:

- List, e.g., a = [1,2.0, "cat"].
- String, e.g., a = "Hello world" or a = 'Hello world' or a = """Hello world""".
- Tuple, e.g., a = (1,2,3).
- Dictionary—collection of pairs key:value, where key is a unique index, e.g., a ={ 1:"cat", 2:"dog", 3:"man"}.

Each object of this collection can be indexed by using square brackets, and indexing starts from zero, e.g.,

```
>>> a=[1,2,3]
>>> a[0]
1
>>> a[1]
2
>>> a[-1]
3
>>> a[-2]
2
```

We can also cut a part of collections using slicing: a[start:stop:step], where start if not appears explicitly is by default the beginning index, i.e., zero, stop is an end index and step is one by default, e.g.,

```
>>> a = [1,2,3,4,5]
>>> a[1:4:2]
[2, 4]
>>> a[:2]
[1, 2]
>>> a[::2]
[1, 3, 5]
```

For strings, the indexing gives selected letter, and for a dictionary, the indexing is by using a key.

Blocks of the code that have specific purposes can be grouped into functions and then called from any place of the program. An example of function definition is

```
>>> def add2(a):
...     return(a+2)
...
```

The function has name add2 and one argument a. It returns the input value increased by two. The use of the function is as follows

```
>>> add2(1)
3
```

that is, the application of the function on the argument one gives three.

One can also define more advanced functions, e.g.,

```
>>> def areaOfRectangle(a, b):
...     area = a*b
...     return(area)
```

which computes the product of its two arguments a and b, stores it in the internal variable area, and returns this value. An example use of the function is as follows

```
>>> areaOfRectangle(2,3)
6
```

Each argument of function can be given a default value, e.g.,

```
>>> def areaOfRectangle2(a, b=1):
...     area = a*b
...     return(area)
```

that can be used in two ways, the first is as before

```
>>> areaOfRectangle2(2,3)
6
```

and the second way uses default value

```
>>> areaOfRectangle2(2)
2
```

where the second argument has the default value one. It is advisable to place the variables with default value at the end of the list of arguments.

One of the basic control flow constructions is if statement, which, in the simplest form, is

```
>>> a=2
>>> if a < 2:
...     print(" a < 2 ")
...     print( "Hello" )
... else:
...     print(" a >= 2 ")
...
 a >= 2
```

Note that the block of case $a < 2$ contains two print statements, and both are indented in the same way. This is important difference of Python and other popular programming language that a new block of code has the same level of indentation. Spaces or tabulation can be used for indentation; however, once chosen, it must be consequently used. IDEs like Spyder helps to preserve correct indentation. Else statement can be omitted.

The iteration can be performed in a few ways. If we must perform iteration when some logical condition is true, then the natural choice is while construction:

```
>>> a = 0
>>> while a < 4:
...     print(a)
...     a = a + 1
...
0
1
2
3
```

In this construction, we set initially a to zero and then in the while loop, if the condition a<4 is fulfilled, then in each turn in the intended block, we print the current value of the variable a and then increment the value in a by one.

Otherwise, if we must iterate over some collection of data, the for loop is better choice:

```
>>> a = [1,2,3]
>>> for i in a:
...     print( i )
...
1
2
3
```

In the loop for the temporary variable i in each cycle, we substitute consecutive elements of the list a and then print them.

```
>>> a = "Hello"
>>> for letter in a :
...     print( letter )
...
H
e
l
l
o
```

Each letter in "Hello" is printed in a new line since print function adds a new line after printing its argument.

Loop over list can be written more economically using functional programming paradigm.[1] The first construct from functional programming is the lambda (or anonymous) function which is usually too simple to give it a name, e.g., the function $f(x) = 2x$ is written as

```
lambda x: 2*x
```

and its application on $x = 2$ is

```
(lambda x: 2*x)(2)
```

We can also substitute the lambda function to a variable:

```
f=lambda x: 2*x
```

and then use this variable as a synonym of the function

```
f(2)
```

The second useful thing is the map (higher order) function that takes some function and a list and produces a list of values of this function on initial list, e.g.,

```
map(lambda x: 2*x, [1,2])    #gives: [2,4]
```

Finally, there is also a simple way of filtering a list using filter function and a predicate.[2] For example, filtering positive values from a list is realised by

```
filter(lambda x: x>0, [-1,0,1])    #gives [1]
```

The power of Python comes from abundance of various libraries. Importing and using the library can be done in a few ways, e.g.,

```
>>> import math
>>> math.pi
3.141592653589793
>>> import math as mmm
>>> mmm.pi
3.141592653589793
>>> from math import pi
>>> pi
3.141592653589793
```

Especially the second version where the math module is imported under a new name mmm.

In data analysis applications, we start analysis from importing libraries. As mentioned earlier, there are standard names under which they are imported:

```
import numpy as np
import pandas as pd
import matplotlib.pyplot as plt
import seaborn as sns
```

It is advisable to have these import lines always on the top of the Python script or Jupyter Notebook.

We describe basic usage of the libraries. The first one is NumPy [19]. It is the library that provides arrays as data structures and fast operations on them. There is, in large abundance, linear algebra operations. The NumPy arrays are used to store in a matrix the data of the same type. The arrays can be initialised using lists as in the following example.

```
>>> import numpy as np
>>> v = np.array([1,2,3])
>>> v
array([1, 2, 3])
>>> v.shape
(3,)
>>> A = np.array([[1,2],[3,4]])
>>> A
array([[1, 2],
       [3, 4]])
>>> A.shape

(2, 2)
>>> A.shape = (4,)
>>> A
array([1, 2, 3, 4])
```

In the previous example, v is a vector—a one-dimensional matrix initialised from the list [1,2,3]. The dimensionality of an array can be checked by the attribute shape that contains the tuple that indicates the number of elements along each dimension. The variable A contains 2×2 matrix of shape (2,2). The last part shows that we can change the 2 by 2 matrix A into a 4-dimensional vector by substituting to its shape the tuple of appropriate dimension.

The arrays can be indexed and sliced as for lists—one indexing for each dimension starting from zero, e.g.,

```
>>> B = np.array([[1,2],[3,4]])
>>> B[1]
array([3, 4])
>>> B[0,0]
1
>>> B[1,0]
3
```

We can also address whole columns and rows using slicing

```
>>> B[:,0]
array([1, 3])
>>> B[:,1]
array([2, 4])
>>> B[0,:]
array([1, 2])
>>> B[1,:]
array([3, 4])
```

As a simple example of plotting using Matplotlib library [22] is as follows

```
>>> import matplotlib.pylab as plt
>>> X=np.arange(0,10,0.01)
>>> X
array([0.  , 0.01, 0.02, 0.03, 0.04, 0.05, 0.06, 0.07, 0.08, 0.09, 0.1 ,
       0.11, 0.12, 0.13, 0.14, 0.15, 0.16, 0.17, 0.18, 0.19, 0.2 , 0.21,
       0.22, 0.23, 0.24, 0.25, 0.26, 0.27, 0.28, 0.29, 0.3 , 0.31, 0.32,
       0.33, 0.34, 0.35, 0.36 ....])
>>> Y = np.sin(X)
>>> plt.plot(X,Y)
[<matplotlib.lines.Line2D object at 0x7f37bbd1b5e0>]
>>> plt.xlabel("x")
Text(0.5, 0, "x")
>>> plt.ylabel("y")

Text(0, 0.5, 'y')
>>> plt.show()
>>> plt.savefig("picture.png")
```

which produces the output in Figure 5.3. np.arange(start, stop, step) creates a vector of values from the start to stop using the step. We substitute the array to the variable X. Then we create the array of the values of the function *sin* for each value in X. Note that we use the *sin* function from the NumPy library since it can take the whole array as an argument. It is called vectorisation and makes the library extremely powerful and fast. If we would use math.sin function from the math library, then we must use some loop to create Y array of *sin* values. The function plot plots the points with coordinates (x, y) in arrays X and Y correspondingly. Then we set the labels of X and Y labels and finally we show it in the graphical window on the screen using plt.show(). The last line shows how to save the image in a file.

The most effective way to use Matplolib is to visit gallery on the webpage of the library [22], select the type of the plot in the gallery and then adjust the code that produced the plot.

The usage of Pandas library [21] will be presented in the next section where, a "hands-on" approach to a basic analysis of specific data is presented.

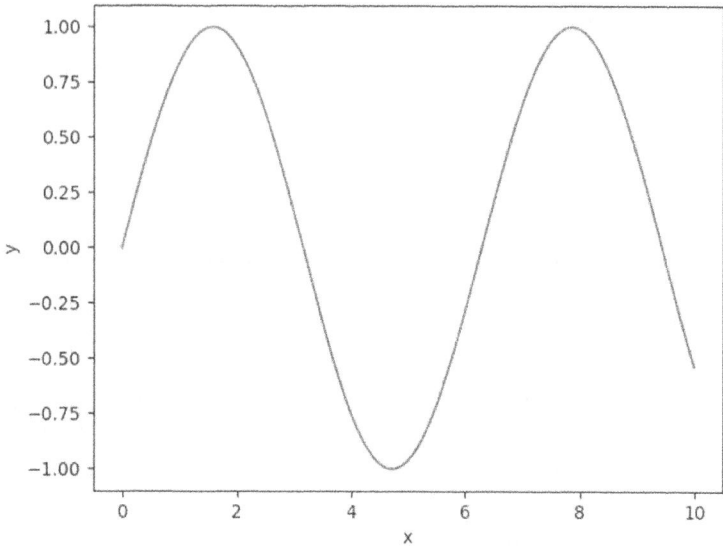

Figure 5.3 Plot of *sin(x)* using Matplotlib library.

5.2 General design pipeline of data analysis

In this paragraph, we introduce models of motivation management in a designer view. We first present the general design pipeline for designing a motivation model. Then we give details of the three first steps such as selecting computational modules, considering reading and cleaning data, and preliminary analysis. We describe how to construct a Python environment for such analysis.

The "preliminary analysis" is mainly the exploratory analysis developed by John W. Tukey. See [7] for more elaborate description of these ideas.

Generally, the pipeline contains the following steps.

1. Read data—in this phase, we read data from external media to a data structure in Python; in our case, we will be reading data from xls (Microsoft® Excel®) format to the DataFrame structure.
2. Cleaning data—checking consistency and treating missing or not defined (e.g., NaN—Not a Number values.
3. Preliminary analysis—this includes basic characteristics that allow help to understand the data and give suggestions on analysis.
4. Construct a model—understanding the data in order to propose a model that describes the data.
5. Prepare the report.

We give general design principles and some background knowledge in this paragraph. We use an example to illustrate the design process of motivation modelling for a specific task in the next chapter.

5.2.1 Reading data

In the beginning, we import libraries useful in later analysis:

```
import numpy as np
import pandas as pd
from pandas import ExcelWriter
from pandas import ExcelFile
import matplotlib.pyplot as plt
import seaborn as sns
import scipy
```

We will be using the data structure called the DataFrame from the Pandas library. It can be imagined as a Python version of a spreadsheet or a matrix. Moreover, it can be indexed similarly to lists.

The DataFrame has an easy method that reads data from xls files:

```
df = pd.read_excel('FILENAME.xlsx', sheetname='Spreadsheet_Name')
```

where FILENAME.xls is the name of the file, and Spreadsheet_Name is the name of spreadsheet with data.

DataFrame also allows importing data from many other formats. The basic one is CSV (comma-separated values), where each record has fields separated by a comma or some other symbol (blank space, tabulation or, e.g., semicolon). This format allows us to interchange data between different systems. The method of reading CSV files is as follows:

```
df = pd.read_csv('FILENAME.csv', sep=",")
```

where the optional argument sep defines how fields in the record are separated. The other options are available by help(pd.read_csv).

We should also check that the reading was correctly done by listing some initial records by

```
df.head()
```

printing the names of columns of the data

```
print(df.columns)
```

Generally, in research on socio-economic problems, especially motivation management, (online) surveys were adopted as a tools for collecting dataset. Usually the survey is divided into parts as each discusses specific information. The survey contains items with questions (labelled by letters, e.g., P1, P2, P3 . . .). As we mentioned, the final version of the structure of the survey should be in the matrix form, where, in the column, there are answers which have numeric values for the questions, split in categories (e.g., P1, P2, P3 . . . or Q1, Q2, . . .). Most often, a five-point Likert scale is used for each part of the survey.

For further use, we create DataFrame of this range.

```
pSelected = df.loc[:,'P1.1':'P6.8'].copy()
```

The first index (here ':'—all) means rows, and the second range 'P1.1': 'P6.8' is for columns. After slicing the original DataFrame, we perform the deep copy by copy() method. Deep copy means that we create independent instance of DataFrame with copy of data. In contrast, shallow copy is a synonym for the reference to the same DataFrame.

5.2.2 Cleaning data

In the second step of the analysis, the problem of the incompleteness of data must be addressed.

We can check the range of the values' data by selecting a column, e.g., P1, with numeric values of answers (e.g., in Likert scale), sorting and taking unique element:

```
sorted(pSelected.loc[:,'P1.1'].unique())
```

In the case of Likert scale, the result of the set of answers is [1,2,3,4,5].

We can check which columns have only numerical values using one of the following constructions:

```
pSelected.isnull().values.any()
pSelected.isnull().any()
pSelected.isnull().sum()
```

In the case the data are clean, containing not many NaN values, one can convert NaN values to, e.g., some value out of the of data range—in our case, it can be, e.g., zero.

```
pSelected.fillna(0,inplace=1)
```

And then again checking if the replacement was successful.

```
pSelected.isnull().values.any()
```

In the case when statistic is large, we can also remove rows which have incomplete rows using:

```
pSelected.dropna(axis=0)
```

where axis = 0 drops rows containing NaN values, and axis = 1 drops columns.

5.2.3 Preliminary analysis

In this section, some tools for preliminary analysis of data will be constructed and used.

Basic correlation

The first simplest operation we can do on data is to plot *correlation plots* between pairs of columns—that means the answer of the selected questions. This average in each group represents "averaged" answer for this group. First we compute averaged values and add them to Selected DataFrame as a new column:

```
pSelected['P1_average' ] = pSelected.loc[:,'P1.1':'P1.18'].mean(axis=1)
pSelected['P2_average' ] = pSelected.loc[:,'P2.2':'P2.18'].mean(axis=1)
pSelected['P3_average' ] = pSelected.loc[:,'P3.1':'P3.8'].mean(axis=1)
pSelected['P4_average' ] = pSelected.loc[:,'P4.1':'P4.8'].mean(axis=1)
pSelected['P5_average' ] = pSelected.loc[:,'P5.1':'P5.20'].mean(axis=1)
pSelected['P6_average' ] = pSelected.loc[:,'P6.1':'P6.8'].mean(axis=1)
```

Then the standard method scattered matrix of DataFrame produces correlation matrix

```
paverageScatterPlot=pd.scatter_matrix(pSelected.loc[:, 'P1_average':'P6_average'], \
alpha =0.5, figsize=(15,15), grid=True)
```

which produces plot from Figure 5.4. Note that '\' in Python indicates a broken line that is continued in the next one.

The second visual tool that helps to note some correlations between data rows is graphical representation of correlation matrix. There are three main approaches to correlation by Pearson, Kendall, and Spearman. The last one is usually used in management and sociology studies. We provide a procedure that calculate correlation matrix and plot it graphically for better visualisation.

```
def cov_matrix(m, method = 'spearman'):
    """Plot correlation matrix and returns it
    method = {pearson, kendall, spearman}
    """

print(m.columns)
cov_data = m.corr(method)
plt.figure(figsize=(20,20))
sns.heatmap(cov_data, cbar=True, cmap= sns.color_palette("cubehelix", 10),
annot=True, square=True, annot_kws={'size':15}, fmt='.2f',
xticklabels= m.columns, yticklabels=m.columns)
return(cov_data)
```

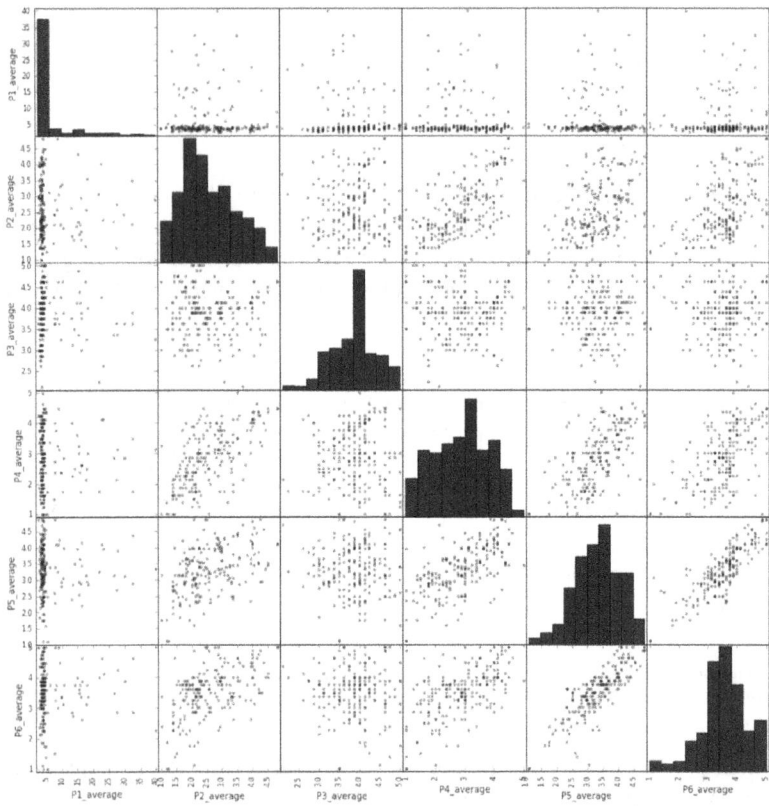

Figure 5.4 Plot of correlation that can show some correlations between some variables. Here the positive correlation between P5_average and P6_average is visible.

The default value of correlation (parameter method) is set to Spearman correlation. As an example, we provide a correlation matrix for the set of P1 group of questions. The code:

```
p1Selected = pSelected.loc[:, 'P1.1':'P1.18'].copy()
p1Selected['P1_average' ] =pSelected.loc[:, 'P1_average'].copy()
p1CorMatrix = cov_matrix(p1Selected)
```

produces the correlation matrix in Figure 5.5. This plot has advantage over standard numerical matrix.

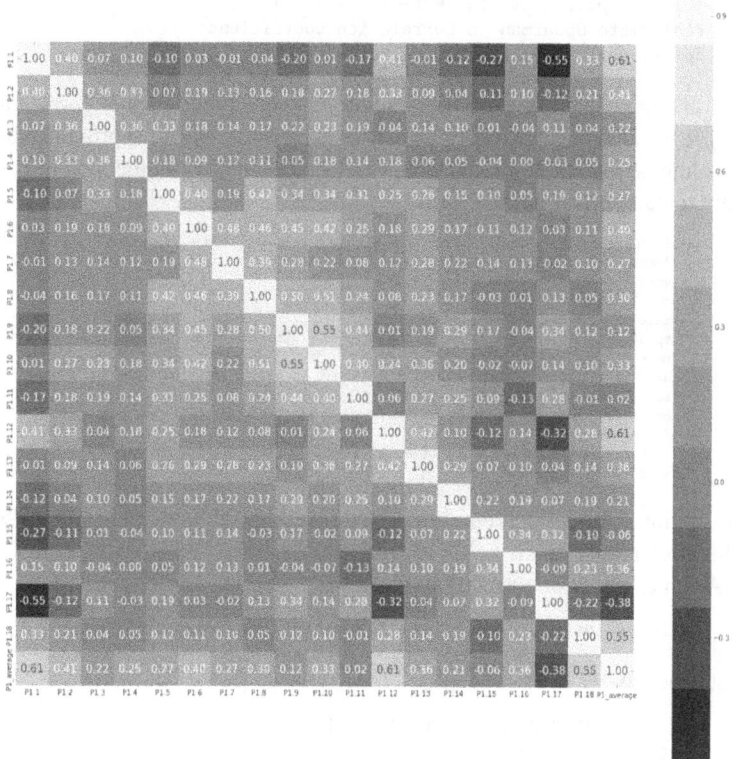

Figure 5.5 Correlation matrix for P1 group of questions.

Advanced correlation

Now we provide a more elaborated framework for searching correlations. We construct the tool that searches for the highest correlation between selected columns in the DataFrame.

We start from the function that calculates the correlation between two rows x1label and x2label in the fulldf DataFrame, namely,

```
def correlator(x1label, x2label, fulldf, method = 'spearman'):
    """Calculate correlation coefficients between two labels x1label and x2label
    method= {pearson, kendall, spearman}
    """
    corrdf = fulldf[[x1label,x2label]].copy()
    cov_data = corrdf.corr(method);
    return(cov_data.iloc[1,0])
```

The use is as follows

```
#full dataset
fulldf = pd.concat([pSelected], axis =1)
#calculate Spearman' s correlation coefficient
correlator("P1.1","P1.2", fulldf)
```

In the next step, we provide function that construct *tuples of correlation coefficient* and the names of rows for this correlation. We must provide labels of columns (the variable 'xlabel'), which correlation with other columns we want to compute. It has the form

```
def fullCorrelation(xlabel,fulldf, removeFirst = False, method = 'spearman'):
    """Make a list of correlation between xlabel column and any other column in dataset
    method= {pearson, kendall, spearman}
    """
    #make list of all possible correlations
    tmpcorr = map( lambda yl: (correlator(xlabel,yl, fulldf, method),yl), fulldf.columns)
    #make a list
    corrList = [(corr, xlabel, ylabel ) for corr, ylabel in tmpcorr ]
    #sort list with respect to the abs(correlation)
    corrListSorted = sorted(corrList, key=lambda tup: np.abs(tup[0]),reverse=True)
    if removeFirst:
        corrListSorted = corrListSorted[1:]
    return(corrListSorted)
```

The option removeFirst removes correlation of the column xlabel with itself which is trivially one.

As an example of correlation, we have

```
fullCorrelation("P6.4", fulldf, removeFirst=True)
```

that produces

```
[(0.63202412337969383, 'P6.4' , u'P6.7'),
 (0.43039545766208398, 'P6.4' , u'P6.1'),
 (0.41625416025732614, 'P6.4' , 'P6_average'),
 (0.40739013687293463, 'P6.4' , u'P2.17'),
 (0.38911994729704052, 'P6.4' , u'P5.15'),
 (0.38354365961709452, 'P6.4' , u'P1.17'),
 ...]
```

The final function makes all possible correlations between columns in a given DataFrame and sort them descending. The code is as follows:

```
def higherCorrelations(fulldf, absLevel=0.7, method = 'spearman'):
    """"Calculate hihest correlation coefficients than absLev on columns in the table
    fulldf method= {pearson, kendall, spearman}
    """
    fullCorrList = map(lambda y: fullCorrelation(y, fulldf, removeFirst=True, \
    method = method), fulldf.columns)
    #flatten list
    import itertools
    flattenList = list(itertools.chain.from_iterable( fullCorrList))
    filtredList = filter (lambda x: np.abs(x[0]) > absLevel, flattenList )
    #sort list with respect to the abs(correlation)
    filterListSorted = sorted(filtredList, key=lambda tup: np.abs(tup[0]),
    reverse=True)
    return(filterListSorted)
```

The procedure uses some basic tools from functional programming described above.

Example is

```
corr = higherCorrelations(fulldf,0.5)
print(corr)
```

which produces

```
[(0.75783681776283485, u'P2.7' , u'P2.8'),
 (0.75783681776283485, u'P2.8' , u'P2.7'),
 (0.72366746344454935, u'P2.9' , u'P.2.10'),
 (0.72366746344454935, u'P.2.10' , u'P2.9'),
 (0.72242809062877178, u'P5.16' , u'P5.17'),
 (0.72242809062877178, u'P5.17' , u'P5.16'),
 ...]
```

The results come in the same pairs since the correlation matrix is symmetric.

This tool allows extracting the highest correlated pairs of rows, which is essential for questionnaires containing too many questions to analyse them item by item. It indicates possible connections between questions.

Principal component analysis

Finally, we present a useful tool called principal component analysis (PCA) [6, 5]. The idea behind the PCA is that the data that carries more variation (are non-constant), carry more information that mostly the constant signal. This allows extracting linear combination of columns that are ordered according to the percent of variation that the combination carries. This has many applications. We indicate two:

- We can reduce the number of variables to those which explain the variation of data the most.
- We can find some linear combination of variables that carries significant variation of the data.

There are standard libraries that perform PCA in Python. We compose them into one useful function

```
def pcaAnalysis(x, scale = True):
    """Perform full PCA analysis and make a plot"""
    #normalizing data before PCA
    if scale:
        from sklearn.preprocessing import StandardScaler
        sc = StandardScaler()
        x = sc.fit_transform(x)
    #PCA
```

```
from sklearn.decomposition import PCA
pca = PCA(n_components = None)
pca.fit(x)
print("Scale = ", scale)
print("Explained variance ratio:", pca.explained_variance_ratio_)
print("Transformation matrix:", pca.components_)
#cumulative sum for PCA
pcaPlot = pd.DataFrame(pca.explained_variance_ratio_,
index=range(1,pca.explained_variance_ratio_.shape[0]+1) ).cumsum().plot(kind='bar' , \
legend=False, grid = True, yticks = np.arange(0.0,1.1,0.1)).set( \
xlabel='Number of components' , ylabel='Explained variance ratio')
return(pca, pcaPlot)
```

This function depends on option scale, the scaling of data to a normal distribution with an average zero and standard deviation one. Then PCA analysis is performed. Then the explained variance (summing to one) of each component is provided, and the transformation matrix to principal components is provided. The tool helps to select some essential principal components and is augmented by the plot of explained variance ration. As an example of application, we have:

```
pcaAnalysis(p3Selected.loc[:,"P3.1":"P3.8"], True)
```

which produces:

```
('Scale = ' , True)
('Explained variance ratio:',
array([ 0.34444514,  0.17280647,  0.13532493,  0.10388899,  0.08342616,
        0.07456051,  0.04712499,  0.03842281]))
('Transformation matrix:',
array([[-0.18855665, -0.09060535, -0.28525785, -0.37925163, -0.449635  ,
        -0.46774202, -0.4413312 , -0.33956702],
       [-0.39544535,  0.66539157,  0.27001208,  0.28170118,  0.1514522 ,
        -0.2764333 , -0.3577708 ,  0.14581451],
       [ 0.59589752,  0.33435109,  0.57760384, -0.30953901, -0.28556298,
        -0.06051046,  0.02696921, -0.13319093],
       [-0.20657143, -0.16852913,  0.35319153,  0.20105306,  0.18296585,
        0.25004728, -0.10621829, -0.81023276],
       [-0.54777078,  0.2642596 ,  0.06732826, -0.60289419, -0.06357289,
        0.29980976,  0.40993671, -0.01113684],
       [ 0.33165248,  0.45913013, -0.53491119, -0.21031343,  0.47725506,
        0.13607413, -0.10795743, -0.30149804],
       [-0.01213037, -0.35786043,  0.31039001, -0.48061576,  0.59868446,
        -0.14914059, -0.33526289,  0.22668944],
       [-0.01050774, -0.01242224,  0.01859997,  0.04325813,  0.26387665,
        -0.71272147,  0.6108298 , -0.21633821]]]))
```

and the plot from Figure 5.6.

This ends the presentation of elementary tools of the initial analysis of (management) data as well as basic Python syntax. The next step is connected with the creation of a model that describes data and has features that were extracted in this chapter. It will be presented in the next chapter.

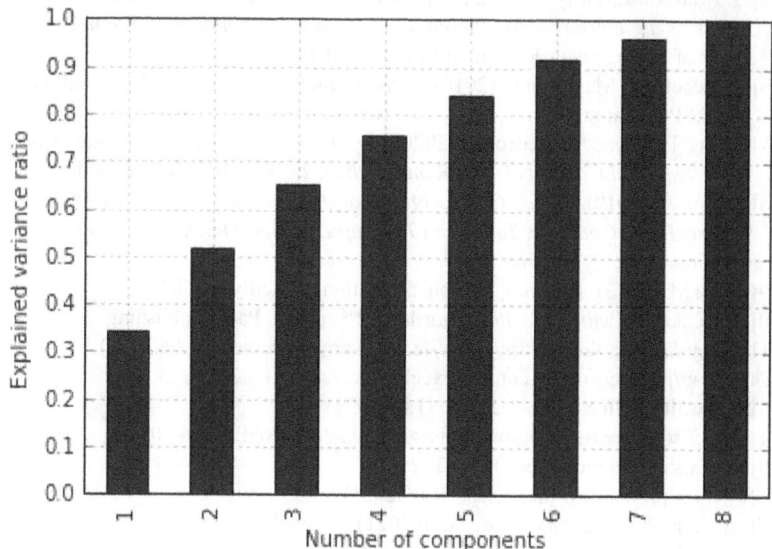

Figure 5.6 Explained variance ration for PCA analysis of P3 set of questions. One can see that first four components explain more than 70% of variance.

Notes

1 Functional programming is an approach to programming using function calls and recursion instead of procedures and iterations. The functions in this approach are 'true' functions as in mathematics, which for a specific input always have the same value.
2 A predicate is a function that returns a logical (boolean) value. It can be used as a filter.

Bibliography

[1] Ozkan M., Solmaz B. (2015), *The changing face of the employees-generation Z and their perception of work*, Procedia Economics and Finance, 26, 476–483.
[2] Hom P.W., Kinicki A.J. (2001), *Toward a greater understanding of how dissatisfaction drives employee turnover*, Academy of Management Journal, 44(5), 975–987.
[3] Harrison D.A., Newman D.A., Roth P.L. (2006), *How important are job attitudes? Meta-analytic Comparisons of integrative behavioral outcomes and time sequences*, Academy of Management Journal, 49(2), 305–325.
[4] Wipulanusat, W., Kokkaew, N., Parnphumeesup, P., & Sunkpho, J. (2019). Exploratory and confirmatory factor analysis of measurement scale for psychological attachment to an organization. WMS Journal of Management, 8(3).

[5] Edwards J.R., Parry M.E. (2017), *On the use of polynomial regression equations as an alternative to difference scores in organizational research*, Academy of Management Journal, 36(6), 1577–1613.

[6] Boschetti A., Massaron L. (2016), *Python Data Science Essentials*, 2nd edition, Packt Publishing.

[7] Bruce P., Bruce A., Gedeck P. (2020), *Practical Statistics for Data Scientists: 50+ Essential Concepts Using R and Python*, 2nd edition, O'Reilly Media.

[8] Géron A. (2019), *Hands-On Machine Learning with Scikit-Learn, Keras, and TensorFlow: Concepts, Tools, and Techniques to Build Intelligent Systems*, 2nd edition, O'Reilly Media.

[9] Lutz M. (2013), *Learning Python*, 5th edition, O'Reilly Media.

[10] Raschka S., *Python Machine Learning*, 2nd edition, Packt Publishing.

[11] *Scipy Lecture Notes*. http://scipy-lectures.org/ (accessed: 11.06.2021).

[12] https://products.office.com/en/excel (accessed: 11.06.2021).

[13] www.libreoffice.org/ (accessed: 11.06.2021).

[14] http://software.dell.com/products/statistica/ (accessed: 11.06.2021).

[15] www.sas.com (accessed: 11.06.2021).

[16] www.r-project.org/ (accessed: 11.06.2021).

[17] www.python.org/ (accessed: 11.06.2021).

[18] https://julialang.org/ (accessed: 11.06.2021).

[19] https://numpy.org/ (accessed: 11.06.2021).

[20] www.scipy.org/ (accessed: 11.06.2021).

[21] https://pandas.pydata.org/ (accessed: 11.06.2021).

[22] https://matplotlib.org/ (accessed: 11.06.2021).

[23] https://seaborn.pydata.org/ (accessed: 11.06.2021).

[24] https://scikit-learn.org/ (accessed: 11.06.2021).

[25] https://ipython.org/ (accessed: 11.06.2021).

[26] www.anaconda.com (accessed: 11.06.2021).

[27] https://python-xy.github.io/ (accessed: 11.06.2021).

[28] https://python-xy.github.io/ (accessed: 11.06.2021).

[29] www.spyder-ide.org/ (accessed: 11.06.2021).

[30] https://jupyter.org/ (accessed: 11.06.2021).

6 The analysis of engagement at the workplace of Generation Z—machine learning in management

Agnieszka Niemczynowicz and
Radosław Antoni Kycia

In this chapter, a hands-on example of analysis of real-world data will be provided. We will design pipeline using machine learning methods. The reader can download the example code from [7] and experiment on his/her own, which we strongly suggest.

The data in analysis are treated as classless, and typical cluster analysis is performed. The data are analyses using Python Library version 0.20.0 installed on Linux operating system. The installation process was described in the previous chapter.

The steps of the processing pipeline consist the following methods (cf. Figure 6.1):

1. Correlation analysis of questions—the first part of analysis which suggests all possible relations between questions. This step should be interpreted with care since the high correlation between questions does not always mean the linear relation.
2. Principal component analysis (PCA)—we perform PCA on standardised data, then we select an optimal number of principal components that explains more than 70% of total variance.
3. Selecting optimal number of clusters—we used k-means classifier on the standardised PCs selected in the previous step. The optimal number of clusters we inferred from elbow method.
4. In order to fix number of clusters in the previous step, we use Bayesian information criterion (BIC) for select optimal Gaussian model in Gaussian mixture model (GMM) from available in Scikit-learn library: spherical, tied, diagonal, and full.

Before we go to the main analysis dataset, we will present an overview of the area of machine learning.

DOI: 10.4324/9781003353935-6

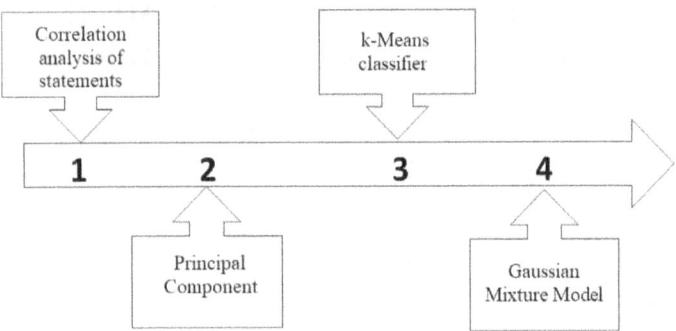

Figure 6.1 Data processing pipeline.

6.1 Machine learning basics

This section starts from an overview of the area of machine learning. The basic idea of ML is to distinguish sets (*decision regions*) in the space of data where data points accumulate. More precisely, we aim at drawing the borders of these sets. The precise characterisation depends on the characteristic of the data. The idea is presented in Figure 6.2.

In general, the variables are called *features*, and data can be organised in a table that each column is a feature. Sometimes, each record (row) has a *class label* that determines to which class the given record belongs.

We distinguish three main disciplines of ML:[1]

- *Supervised learning*—in this case we have features and labels. The task is to distinguish decision regions for each label.
- *Unsupervised learning*—in this case the labels are not provided. We have to distinguish clusters of data that determine decision regions.
- *Regression*—fitting a model—a function with parameters to be determined in fitting. Regression can be seen as a kind of supervised learning with labels that are real numbers.

Currently, there are plenty of good books introducing an accessible way to ML discipline, e.g., [5, 1, 4].

In general, working with specific ML model consists of two steps:

1. Fit/train the model to data. In this step, decision regions are determined.
2. Predict labels for new data.

The essential ingredient is also a validation of the model that is described in length in [5, 1, 4].

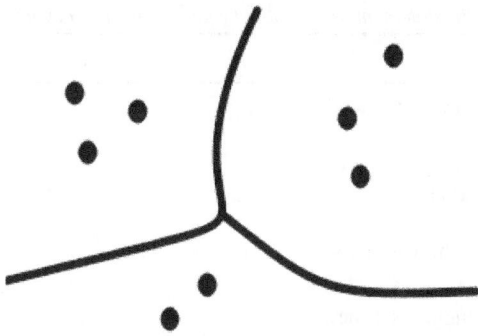

Figure 6.2 Clustering of data and borders of decision regions.

In the below example, we will try to find some characteristics in the answers for a questionnaire/survey with no class labels. In this case we will use a few methods for unsupervised learning to show the grouping of the data.

The following paragraphs will present an illustration of the whole process of design pipeline that was proposed in the previous chapter for motivation management . The description of the analysis and Python code will be provided. The example Jupyter Notebook with the sample can be downloaded from [7]. The specific research problem was described in detail in [3].

6.1.1 The problem

The problem at hand is the analysis of employee motivations for Generation Z. The questionnaire for this part is presented in Table 6.1.

Directions: Please indicate your answer by ticking the appropriate number. The higher level, the more important the modern systems and concepts of remuneration and motivation.

The survey was performed on the Internet using the Qualtrics tool QMETRICS. The sample analysed below consists of the answers of 200 participants from Generation Z. See [3] for details. Further, the consecutive steps of the analysis are presented.

6.1.2 Reading data

The first step is to import necessary libraries:

```
import numpy as np
import pandas as pd
from pandas import ExcelWriter
from pandas import ExcelFile
import matplotlib.pyplot as plt
import seaborn as sns
```

Table 6.1 Part of questionnaire that was used in analysis.

Q3: *Do you agree with the statements below about your engagement at your workplace?*

	1	2	3	4	5
Q5.1. I'm very satisfied with the work I do.	☐	☐	☐	☐	☐
Q5.2. My job is interesting.	☐	☐	☐	☐	☐
Q5.3. I know exactly what I'm expected to do.	☐	☐	☐	☐	☐
Q5.4. I am prepared to show initiative to do my work well.	☐	☐	☐	☐	☐
Q5.5. My job is challenging (sets new goals, is prospective).	☐	☐	☐	☐	☐
Q5.6. I have plenty of freedom in how to do my work.	☐	☐	☐	☐	☐
Q5.7. I get plenty of opportunities to learn in this job.	☐	☐	☐	☐	☐
Q5.8. The facilities/equipment/tools provided are excellent.	☐	☐	☐	☐	☐
Q5.9. I have a lot of support from my boss.	☐	☐	☐	☐	☐
Q5.10. My boss recognises my work.	☐	☐	☐	☐	☐
Q5.11. The experience I am getting now will be of great help in advancing my future career.	☐	☐	☐	☐	☐
Q5.12. I find it easy to keep up with the demands of my job.	☐	☐	☐	☐	☐
Q5.13. I have no problems in achieving balance between my professional and private life.	☐	☐	☐	☐	☐
Q5.14. I like working with my boss.	☐	☐	☐	☐	☐
Q5.15. I get on well with my work colleagues.	☐	☐	☐	☐	☐
Q5.16. I think this organisation is a great place to work.	☐	☐	☐	☐	☐
Q5.17. I believe I have a great future in this organisation.	☐	☐	☐	☐	☐
Q5.18. I intend to go on working for this organisation.	☐	☐	☐	☐	☐
Q5.19. I am happy about the values of this organisation—how it conducts its business.	☐	☐	☐	☐	☐
Q5.20. The products/services provided by this organisation are excellent.	☐	☐	☐	☐	☐

(Note: 1 → I fully disagree 2 → I don't agree 3 → I'm not sure 4 → I agree 5 → I fully agree)

Then the data from the Excel spreadsheet "data.xlsx", from the sheet "Q5", and without header, is read to a DataFrame by:

```
df = pd.read_excel("data.xlsx", sheet_name='Q5' , header=0)
```

The data are read by the standard function read_excel from the Pandas library imported under the name pd. The data are stored in a DataFrame df of Pandas library.

Then we can check if the DataFrame pd was correctly read, namely, the command

```
df.head()
```

provides output from Figure 6.3.

The name of the columns of df can be obtained by

```
df.columns
```

which produces

```
Index(['Q5.1' , 'Q5.2' , 'Q5.3' , 'Q5.4' , 'Q5.5' , 'Q5.6' , 'Q5.7' , 'Q5.8' , 'Q5.9',
       'Q5.10' , 'Q5.11' , 'Q5.12' , 'Q5,13' , 'Q5.14' , 'Q5.15' , 'Q5.16' , 'Q5.17',
       'Q5.18' , 'Q5.19' , 'Q5.20'],
      dtype='object')
```

For further manipulation, it is advised to make a deep (true) copy of the data to a new data frame by invoking copy() method:

```
df_Q5 = df.loc[:,"Q5.1":"Q5.20"].copy()
```

We located columns from the range "Q5.1" through "Q5.20" and then make a deep copy.

One can check if the copy was made properly by listing some initial records:

```
df_Q5.head()
```

	Q5.1	Q5.2	Q5.3	Q5.4	Q5.5	Q5.6	Q5.7	Q5.8	Q5.9	Q5.10	Q5.11	Q5.12	Q5,13	Q5.14	Q5.15	Q5.16	Q5.17	Q5.18
0	3	3	4	4	3	3	2	4	4	3	1	3	4	4	3	4	2	2
1	5	4	3	4	3	3	5	4	5	5	5	3	3	5	5	4	4	4
2	3	3	5	4	3	1	5	3	5	5	3	4	2	5	4	3	1	3
3	3	4	5	5	3	5	3	5	4	4	4	5	5	5	5	4	3	3
4	3	4	4	4	4	3	4	4	3	3	3	4	4	4	4	4	4	3

Figure 6.3 A data frame read from the file.

that should produce the same output as in Figure 6.3.

6.1.3 Cleaning data

Now we check the integrity of the data by the following code:

```
df_Q5.isnull().values.any()
```

checking if there are some fields with NaN (Not a Number) values. In our case the result is false, so the data are clean, and we do not need to make additional corrections.

6.1.4 Correlation analysis

In the next step, the correlation between questions (columns) will be checked. They can help to identify some relations between answers for different questions within the engagement group of questions.

First, we define a function that calculates and visualises correlation matrix (note indentation):

```
def cov_matrix(m, method = 'spearman'):
    """Plot covariance matrix and returns it
    method = {'pearson' , 'kendall' , 'spearman'}
    """
    print(m.columns)
    cov_data = m.corr(method)
    plt.figure(figsize=(20,20))
    sns.heatmap(cov_data, cbar=True, cmap= sns.color_palette("cubehelix", 10), \
    annot=True, square=True, annot_kws={'size':15}, fmt='.2f' , \
    xticklabels= m.columns, yticklabels=m.columns)
    return(cov_data)
```

Then we use this function for our data frame in the following lines:

```
CorMatrix = cov_matrix(df_Q5)
plt.savefig("Q5CorrelationMatrix.png")
```

which produces (by default) Spearman correlation matrix from Figure 6.4 and saves it with the file name Q5CorrelationMatrix.png.

From the plot, it is immediately visible that a group of the last four questions $Q5.16$–$Q5.20$ are correlated among themselves and with questions $Q5.1$–$Q5.2$. These questions (see Table 6.1) measure general satisfaction from the job. There are also other highly correlated questions (above 50%), e.g., between

$Q5.9$ and $Q5.10$ that describe relation with the boss. These correlations are intuitive and can also be used as a sanity check.

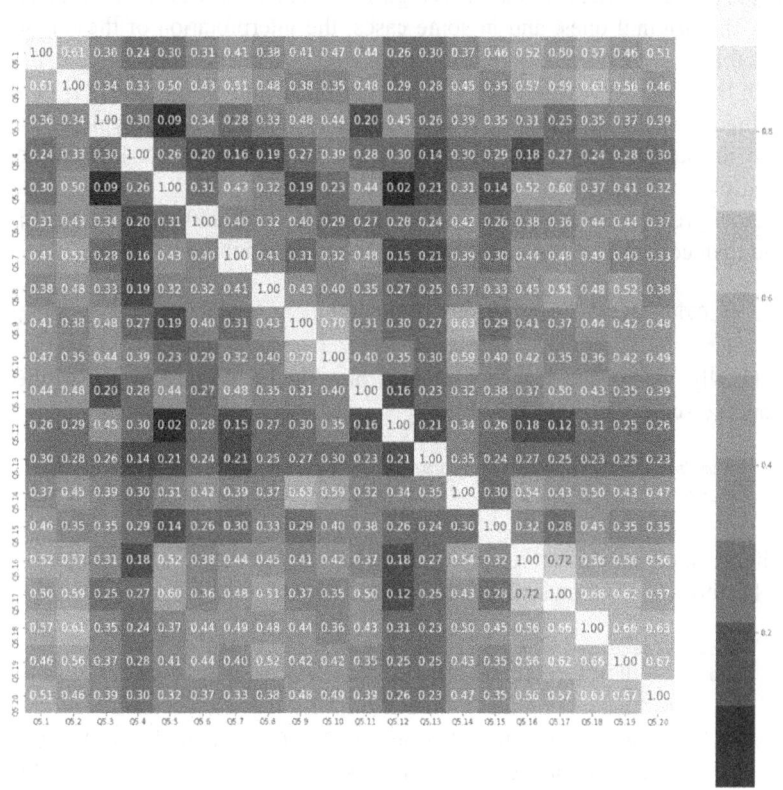

Figure 6.4 Spearman correlation matrix for *Q*5.

The correlation is only a rough suggestion of how data are grouping. More advanced methods from machine learning will be applied in the following sections to represent the grouping of answers for questions. Their aim is distinguishing various clusters that suggest similarities between questions.

6.1.5 Principal component analysis

The first step of analysis is possible dimensionality reduction that will be made in terms of principal component analysis [2]. This is a standard initial transformation in machine learning [5, 1].

Without going into details (see, e.g., [2]), the idea of PCA is to make a linear transformation of data (here on the columns of survey) to the coordinate system where axes carry the highest variations (in decreasing order). The method bases on the intuitive observation that the higher variation of the signal carries more information, as Figure 6.5 suggests. These new variables mix the original ones, and in some cases, the interpretation of these new variables can be proposed depending on described phenomena.

In the first step, scaling the data to zero mean and unit variance is performed to deal with the same "scale" for each column. This is a typical first step in machine learning and prevents ML algorithms to got lost due to multiple scales carried by different columns.

As a preparation for PCA, first we transpose our DataFrame calling T} and then copy transposed DataFrame to the new variable df_Q5 by

```
df_Q5T = df_Q5.T.copy(); df_Q5T.head()
```

Finally, we print a few first rows as presented in Figure 6.6. Then the standard scaling is performed by

```
from sklearn.preprocessing import StandardScaler
df_st =  StandardScaler().fit_transform(df_Q5T)
```

where scaled data are stored under df_st.

Performing PCA on scaled data requires only two lines

```
from sklearn.decomposition import PCA
pca_out = PCA().fit(df_st)
```

where, in the second line, the PCA object (PCA()) is created, and then the fit(. . .) method is applied, which creates the PCA transformation for specific data stored in df_st variable.

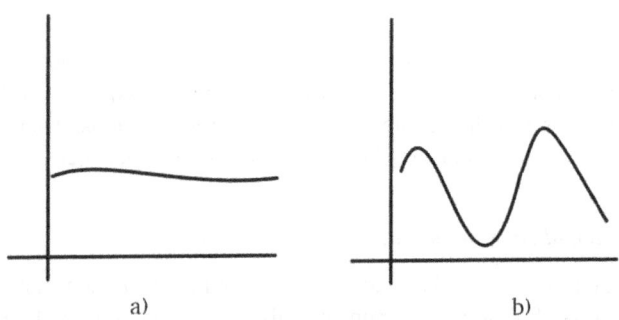

a)   b)

Figure 6.5 Intuitively, "flat signal" a) carries less information than those with more "dynamics" b).

	0	1	2	3	4	5	6	7	8	9	...	190	191	192	193	194	195	196	197	198	199
Q5.1	3	5	3	3	3	2	4	4	1	3	...	4	3	3	3	4	2	3	2	1	1
Q5.2	3	4	3	4	4	1	4	3	1	4	...	2	4	5	3	2	3	4	1	5	4
Q5.3	4	3	5	5	4	4	5	5	3	4	...	2	4	5	3	2	3	4	2	5	5
Q5.4	4	4	4	5	4	4	3	3	1	4	...	3	4	5	4	2	2	4	3	5	4
Q5.5	3	3	3	3	4	1	3	4	1	3	...	4	4	5	4	4	4	5	4	5	5

5 rows × 200 columns

Figure 6.6 Transposition of df *Q5*.

The next step is to extract vital information that characterise PCA model. The following code:

```
print("Explained variance ratio = ", pca_out.explained_variance_ratio_)
print("Explained variance (eigenvalues) = ", pca_out.explained_variance_)
print("Cumulative sum = ", np.cumsum(pca_out.explained_variance_ratio_))
```

produces

```
Explained variance ratio =  [2.17797771e-01 9.92819512e-02
7.46577769e-02 6.94343593e-02 6.68968814e-02 5.47357588e-02
5.26694959e-02 4.96076113e-02 4.36607429e-02 3.92880197e-02
3.52773558e-02 3.19774077e-02 3.04258514e-02 2.96470197e-02
2.66644542e-02 2.39750826e-02 2.02341390e-02 1.82762794e-02
1.54920422e-02 2.17690131e-32]
Explained variance (eigenvalues) =  [4.53936406e+01 2.06924488e+01
1.55602525e+01 1.44715823e+01 1.39427184e+01 1.14080845e+01
1.09774318e+01 1.03392706e+01 9.09981799e+00 8.18845042e+00
7.35254363e+00 6.66476497e+00 6.34138798e+00 6.17906306e+00
5.55743362e+00 4.99691196e+00 4.21722054e+00 3.80916139e+00
3.22886774e+00 4.53712063e-30]


Cumulative sum =  [0.21779777 0.31707972 0.3917375  0.46117186
 0.52806874 0.5828045  0.63547399 0.68508161 0.72874235 0.76803037
 0.80330772 0.83528513 0.86571098 0.895358   0.92202246 0.94599754
 0.96623168 0.98450796 1.         1.         ]
```

The essential information is carried by the cumulative sum of explained variances for principal components (PCs). One can note that the sum of explained variance ratios for nine components is above 72%. Typically, the cumulative sum above 70% is considered to be sufficient.

The graphical interpretation can be obtained by running:

```
plt.grid(True)
plt.step(range(1,len(pca_out.explained_variance_ratio_)+1), \
np.cumsum(pca_out.explained_variance_ratio_), where='mid' , \
color='red' , label='Cumulative distribution')
plt.xlabel("Principal component")
plt.ylabel("Explained variance ratio")
plt.bar(range(1,len(pca_out.explained_variance_ratio_)+1),pca_out.explained_variance_ratio_)
plt.legend()
plt.savefig("pca.png")
```

that produces the plot in Figure 6.7 that is saved in pca.png file. Taking this into account, in further analysis, first nine PCs will be used.

In order to prepare a DataFrame with PC vs. questions labels (scores for PCA), we run the following code:

```
scores=PCA(n_components=9).fit_transform(df_st)

num_pc = pca_out.n_features_
cols =["PC"+str(i) for i in list(range(1, 10))]
df_scores=pd.DataFrame(scores, columns = cols, index=df_Q5T.index)
df_scores
```

which constructs df_scores data frame presented in Figure 6.8. That matrix provides the correspondence between PCs and questions. The method

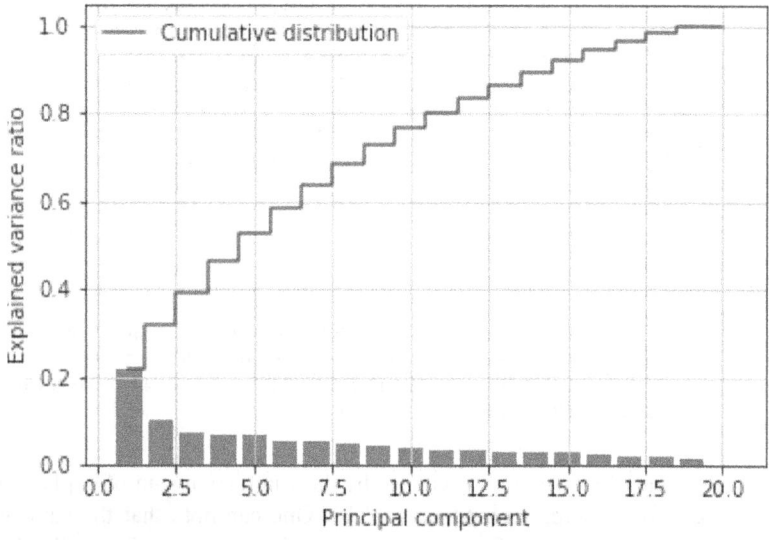

Figure 6.7 Cumulative sum for explained variance ratios for *Q*5.

	PC1	PC2	PC3	PC4	PC5	PC6	PC7	PC8	PC9
Q5.1	-1.072508	-0.205395	-3.744323	-2.548834	-5.214509	-3.230973	6.002138	-1.732583	-4.654623
Q5.2	0.539856	4.381662	-1.296618	1.461805	-1.195015	-1.427036	2.067605	-1.795215	-4.610541
Q5.3	-9.434172	-2.959422	0.283085	2.301236	-0.203073	0.023097	-2.963912	-4.448509	-0.086511
Q5.4	-12.190105	3.851061	-3.845692	-1.400164	1.896829	-1.532640	-4.523083	0.570390	-0.615326
Q5.5	2.420341	11.040246	0.282513	-0.075163	7.920347	1.162162	-0.918652	-1.546126	-0.590189
Q5.6	2.222431	-0.270571	4.192161	10.400137	2.130560	-7.234127	1.477259	5.545999	-0.323676
Q5.7	4.662478	4.817740	10.536602	-0.510792	-6.061730	-1.149040	-1.717454	-6.025343	2.884440
Q5.8	4.775332	-2.571513	3.034487	2.171818	-3.331634	8.735359	-3.869955	3.083605	-4.133780
Q5.9	1.241159	-9.359327	4.635144	-3.275167	3.854318	-1.677873	0.231792	0.072244	-1.511283
Q5.10	-1.802763	-6.516394	1.977409	-5.679006	2.834638	-0.776718	-1.003776	0.942674	-0.423754
Q5.11	1.078349	6.273068	2.013666	-8.478055	-1.397613	-1.649695	-0.430706	6.964334	2.091437
Q5.12	-8.484684	-0.101190	-0.430150	3.047781	-1.756650	2.107388	-2.987103	3.080188	-1.960978
Q5,13	-7.674070	0.073352	1.282243	2.253755	0.557193	6.423755	8.883074	1.466386	5.885487
Q5.14	-1.813430	-3.547096	2.606910	-2.032879	5.057454	-0.810438	1.548461	-2.244098	0.244141
Q5.15	-9.673821	0.536800	-1.654180	-0.621523	-5.121664	-0.364441	0.320384	0.684649	0.482115
Q5.16	2.761785	0.474692	-2.540860	1.234092	3.046170	1.992303	2.170933	-4.438071	-2.362218
Q5.17	13.473749	0.753643	-3.061074	-0.826653	2.218792	2.873957	0.916433	1.429212	-1.096276
Q5.18	9.665149	-2.196495	-3.912901	-0.705799	-4.693951	-2.010078	0.877754	0.615608	0.804627
Q5.19	6.715757	-1.682706	-4.286014	3.071195	-1.014041	-0.155071	-3.957770	-1.033931	4.312489
Q5.20	2.589166	-2.792156	-6.072409	0.212216	0.473578	-1.299892	-2.123422	-1.191411	5.664420

Figure 6.8 PC scores for *Q5*.

fit_transform(. . .) trains the PCA model and then transforms data into PC space. The list \texttt{cols} made on the fly contains strings of the form "PC1" to "PC9", and it is used to initialise names of columns for the DataFrame df_scores.

The final part of this section is to visualise relation from Figure 6.8. We will use a 3D plot and project to the first three PCs. This task is made by the following:

```
from matplotlib import pyplot
from mpl_toolkits.mplot3d import Axes3D
from numpy.random import rand
from pylab import figure

fig = figure()

fig = plt.figure(figsize=plt.figaspect(0.5)*1.5)
ax = fig.gca(projection='3d')
```

```
ax = Axes3D(fig)

for i in range(len(scores[:,0])):
    ax.scatter(scores[i,0],scores[i,1],scores[i,2],color='b' , s=100)
    ax.text(scores[i,0],scores[i,1],scores[i,2],  '%s' % (df_scores.index[i]),\
    size=15, zorder=1,  color='k')

plt.grid(True)
ax.set_xlabel("PC1 ({:.1f}%)".format(pca_out.explained_variance_ratio_[0]*100))
ax.set_ylabel("PC2 ({:.1f}%)".format(pca_out.explained_variance_ratio_[1]*100))
ax.set_zlabel("PC3 ({:.1f}%)".format(pca_out.explained_variance_ratio_[2]*100))

plt.savefig("pca9-3dim.png")
```

The for loop iterates over rows of table from Figure 6.8 and plot the point with coordinates [$PC1$, $PC2$, $PC3$], i.e., with three first coordinates carried the largest explained variance. In addition, `ax.text(...)` add annotation— $Q5$ label of each question at the marked point. The figure is saved in pca9–3dim.png and is presented in Figure 6.9.

Even in a 3D plot, one can note some grouping of points into clusters. This grouping can be analysed in terms of k-means and Gaussian mixture models presented in the following sections.

6.1.6 k-means model

The k-means algorithm aims at constructing k clusters from the set of $N \geq k$ points. In each cluster, variance of points is minimised.

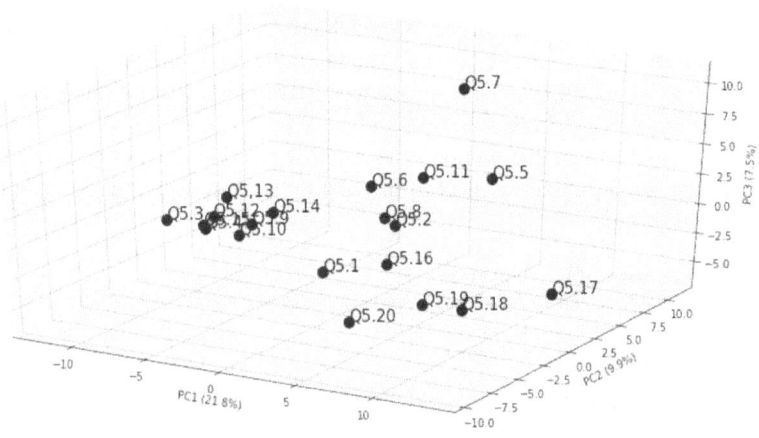

Figure 6.9 PC components for $Q5$ projected to the 3D space spanned by first three PCs.

Estimation of an optimal number of clusters is made on the plot of the sum of square distance (SSE) between member points of a cluster and centroids
(centers) of the cluster using the following code:

```
from sklearn.cluster import KMeans

kmeans_kwargs = {"init": "random", "n_init": 10,  "max_iter": 300, "random_state": 42}
sse = []
for k in range(1, 21):
    kmeans = KMeans(n_clusters=k, **kmeans_kwargs)
    kmeans.fit(scores)
    sse.append(kmeans.inertia_)

plt.grid()
plt.plot(range(1, 21), sse)
plt.xticks(range(1, 21))
plt.xlabel("Number of Clusters")
plt.ylabel("SSE")

plt.savefig("kMenasPCA9-3dimScree.png")
```

In for loop, the iteration over the number of clusters is made, and in each turn, the k-means object is created kMeans, the model is fitted, and then SSE is stored in SSE array. Then it is plotted, and the plot is saved in the file kMenasPCA9–3dimScree.png. The plot is presented in Figure 6.10.

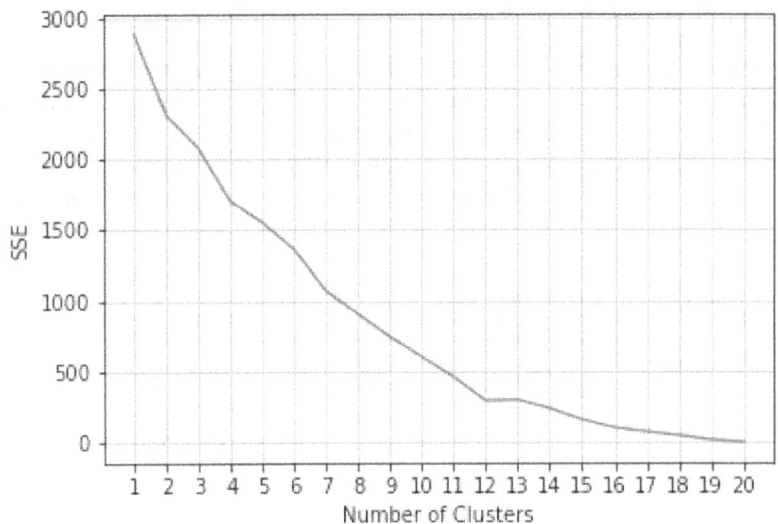

Figure 6.10 SSE plot for *Q*5.

To estimate the optimal number of clusters, we use the elbow rule. The plot decreases from 3000 to about 1000 for clusters ranging from 1–8 and then in the range of 8–20 by only 1000; therefore, the elbow point is 7–8. Note that this technique non-uniquely determines the best choice, and some additional reasoning is needed. One can also choose 12 clusters where a small plateau is visible. However, in the following analysis, we use eight clusters as a minimal value. One can note that other methods of estimating an optimal number of clusters are also at our disposal [5, 1].

Fixing number of clusters on eight, we analyse the grouping of questions using the following code:

```
from sklearn.cluster import KMeans
kmeans = KMeans(8, random_state=0)
labels = kmeans.fit_predict(scores.T[0:3].T)
print("Labels = ", labels)
print("etiquettes = ", df_scores.index)
print("clusters = ", list(zip(labels,df_scores.index)))
```

that prints:

```
Labels =  [7 3 1 6 3 5 2 5 4 4 3 1 1 4 1 7 0 0 0 7]
etiquettes =  Index(['Q5.1' , 'Q5.2' , 'Q5.3' , 'Q5.4' , 'Q5.5',
       'Q5.6' , 'Q5.7' , 'Q5.8' , 'Q5.9' , 'Q5.10' , 'Q5.11' , 'Q5.12',
       'Q5.13' , 'Q5.14' , 'Q5.15' , 'Q5.16' , 'Q5.17' , 'Q5.18' , 'Q5.19',
       'Q5.20'], dtype='object')
clusters =  [(7, 'Q5.1'), (3, 'Q5.2'), (1, 'Q5.3'), (6, 'Q5.4'), (3, 'Q5.5'),
 (5, 'Q5.6'), (2, 'Q5.7'), (5, 'Q5.8'), (4, 'Q5.9'), (4, 'Q5.10'), (3, 'Q5.11'),
 (1, 'Q5.12'), (1, 'Q5.13'), (4, 'Q5.14'), (1, 'Q5.15'), (7, 'Q5.16'),
 (0, 'Q5.17'), (0, 'Q5.18'), (0, 'Q5.19'), (7, 'Q5.20')]
```

The method zip create the pairs from corresponding elements of list labels and df_scores.index that is associate with each $Q5$ index its class. It is an extremely effective programming trick.

The cluster content, for better visibility, is presented in Table 6.2. The content of clusters can be interpreted as a set of questions that can be grouped.

Table 6.2 k-means clusters for $Q5$.

Cluster number	Members
0	Q5.17, Q5.18, Q5.19
1	Q5.3, Q5.12, Q5.13, Q5.15
2	Q5.7
3	Q5.2, Q5.5, Q5.11
4	Q5.9, Q5.10, Q5.14
5	Q5.6, Q5.8
6	Q5.4
7	Q5.1, Q5.16, Q5.20

For instance, from Table 6.2, the cluster zero connects the questions about the plans for continuing working in the organisation and satisfaction with values the company provides. The cluster one shows that precise description of job responsibilities allows employee allows to achieve work-life balance and induces a good atmosphere at the workplace. For a detailed analysis, see [3].

The plot of clusters projected on the space spanned by the first three PCs is realised by the code:

```python
from matplotlib import pyplot
from mpl_toolkits.mplot3d import Axes3D
from numpy.random import rand
from pylab import figure

fig = figure()

fig = plt.figure(figsize=plt.figaspect(0.5)*1.5)

ax = fig.gca(projection='3d')
ax = Axes3D(fig)

for i in range(len(scores[:,0])):
    ax.text(scores[i,0],scores[i,1],scores[i,2],  '%s' % (df_scores.index[i]), \
    size=15,zorder=1,  color='k')

ax.scatter(scores[:,0],scores[:,1],scores[:,2], c=labels, s=200, cmap='viridis')

plt.grid(True)
ax.set_xlabel("PC1 ({:.1f}%)".format(pca_out.explained_variance_ratio_[0]*100))
ax.set_ylabel("PC2 ({:.1f}%)".format(pca_out.explained_variance_ratio_[1]*100))
ax.set_zlabel("PC3 ({:.1f}%)".format(pca_out.explained_variance_ratio_[2]*100))

centers = kmeans.cluster_centers_
ax.scatter(centers[:, 0], centers[:, 1], centers[:, 2], c='red' , marker='+' , s=300, \
alpha=0.5, label="Cluster center");
ax.legend(loc="lower left")

plt.savefig("kMansPCA9-3dim.png")
```

and the figure saved in the file kMansPCA9–3dim.png is presented in Figure 6.11.

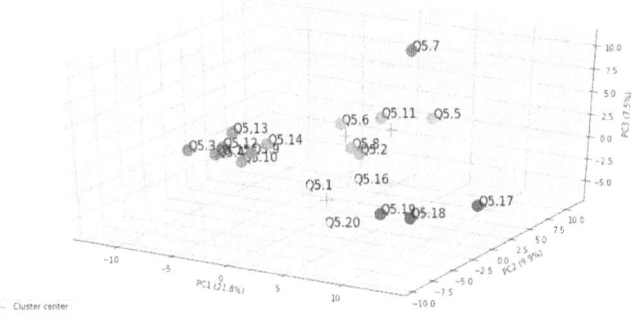

Figure 6.11 K-means clusters for *Q*5 projected to the first three PC axes.

The coordinates of the centroids are extracted from the model by invoking `kmeans.cluster_centers`.

6.1.7 Gaussian mixture model

As a different approach to clustering, we present the Gaussian mixture model [1], which represents cluster division of the whole data space as a linear combination of Gaussian distributions. The algorithm needs a set of initial clusters.

By default, the algorithm from Scikit-learn [6] uses the input from the k-means algorithm. We will use this default setup since we used the k-means algorithm in the previous section.

There are four options available for Gaussian covariance matrix in GMM available in Scikit-learn library [6]:

- Spherical—diagonal with all diagonal elements equal.
- Diag—diagonal covariance matrix.
- Tied—all Gaussians share the same covariance matrix.
- Full—general independent covariance matrices for each component.

One way to select the best model is to use the Bayesian information criterion (BIC). So, first, we fix the number of clusters to eight from the previous section and then select the model that minimises the BIC measure.

The code scoring GMM for the optimal BIC is:

```
from sklearn import mixture
import itertools
from scipy import linalg

X = scores

lowest_bic = np.infty
bic = []
n_components_range = range(1, 21)
cv_types = ['spherical' , 'tied' , 'diag' , 'full']
for cv_type in cv_types:
    for n_components in n_components_range:
        # Fit a Gaussian mixture with EM
        gmm = mixture.GaussianMixture(n_components=n_components, \
        covariance_type=cv_type)
        gmm.fit(X)
        bic.append(gmm.bic(X))
        if bic[-1] < lowest_bic:
            lowest_bic = bic[-1]
            best_gmm = gmm

bic = np.array(bic)
color_iter = itertools.cycle(['navy' , 'turquoise' , 'cornflowerblue',
                            'darkorange'])
```

```
clf = best_gmm
bars = []

# Plot the BIC scores
plt.figure(figsize=(8, 6))

spl = plt.subplot(2, 1, 1)
for i, (cv_type, color) in enumerate(zip(cv_types, color_iter)):
    xpos = np.array(n_components_range) + .2 * (i - 2)
    bars.append(plt.bar(xpos, bic[i * len(n_components_range):
                                    (i + 1) * len(n_components_range)],
                        width=.2, color=color))
plt.xticks(n_components_range)
plt.ylim([bic.min() * 1.01 - .01 * bic.max(), bic.max()])
plt.title('BIC score per model')
xpos = np.mod(bic.argmin(), len(n_components_range)) + .65 +\
    .2 * np.floor(bic.argmin() / len(n_components_range))
spl.set_xlabel('Number of components')
spl.legend([b[0] for b in bars], cv_types)

plt.savefig("BICScorePCA9 - 3dim.png")
```

It was adapted from the Scikit-learn library documentation.[2] The change is in the line X = scores, where we set the data to our score data frame in the for loop where the proper range (from 1 to 21) was set for our data, and at the end, where we save the plot under the name BICScorePCA9–3dim.png .

The plot is presented in Figure 6.12. One can note that for eight clusters, the minimal value of BIC appears for the "full" model. This value will be used in the next part for specific calculations.

The parameters of Gaussian can be obtained by the following code:

```
from sklearn.mixture import GaussianMixture
gm = GaussianMixture(n_components=8,covariance_type='full' , random_state=0).fit(X)

print("means of gaussian model = \n", gm.means_)
```

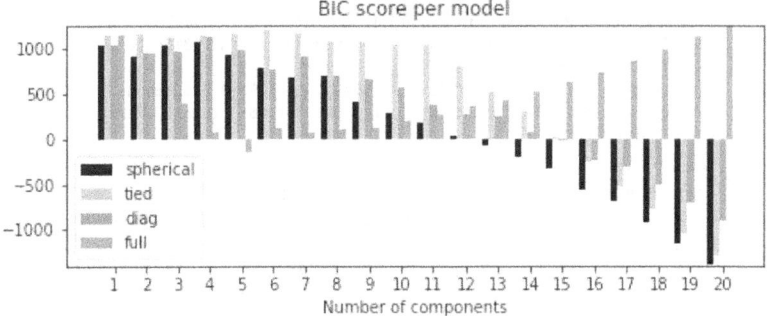

Figure 6.12 BIC score for *Q*5.

```
print("weights of each mixture = \n", gm.weights_)
print("covariance matrices = \n", gm.covariances_)
print("convergent = ", gm.converged_)
```

which produces rather long output that was trimmed:

```
means of gaussian model =
[[-7.67407002  0.07335233  1.28224272  2.25375459  0.55719339  6.42375474
   8.88307436  1.46638564  5.88548653]
 [13.47374927  0.7536434  -3.06107357 -0.82665287  2.21879172  2.87395672
   0.91643269  1.4292119  -1.0962763 ]
 [ 5.93635072 -2.31071747 -2.8092091   1.1873574  -2.14151189  1.31757969
  -2.26834818  0.36846761  1.66193902]
 [-0.79167798 -6.4742725   3.0731543  -3.66235051  3.91546991 -1.08834286
   0.25882574 -0.40972652 -0.5636319 ]
 [-9.94569525  0.33181217 -1.41173416  0.83183263 -1.29613961  0.05835093
  -2.53842834 -0.02832066 -0.54517508]
 [ 2.22243122 -0.27057115  4.19216114 10.40013743  2.13056049 -7.23412728
   1.47725931  5.54599871 -0.32367626]
 [ 1.8623905   4.10178915  0.64746276 -0.08777856 -0.30094732 -0.53051669
   1.52091376 -3.10746776 -1.86662613]
 [ 1.07834907  6.27306838  2.01366612 -8.47805494 -1.3976127  -1.64969461
  -0.43070624  6.96433429  2.09143663]]
weights of each mixture =
[0.05 0.05 0.2  0.15 0.2  0.05 0.25 0.05]
covariance matrices =
[[[ 1.00000000e-06 -2.81031697e-30 -4.87121609e-29 -8.24359646e-29
   -2.06089911e-29 -2.39813715e-28 -3.29743858e-28 -5.62063395e-29
   -2.24825358e-28]
  [-2.81031697e-30  1.00000000e-06  4.80712114e-31  8.13512809e-31
    2.03378202e-31  2.36658272e-30  3.25405123e-30  5.54667824e-31
    2.21867130e-30]
  [-4.87121609e-29  4.80712114e-31  1.00000000e-06  1.41008887e-29
    3.52522217e-30  4.10207671e-29  5.64035547e-29  9.61424228e-30
    3.84569691e-29]
  [-8.24359646e-29  8.13512809e-31  1.41008887e-29  1.00000000e-06
    5.96576060e-30  6.94197597e-29  9.54521695e-29  1.62702562e-29
    6.50810247e-29]
  [-2.06089911e-29  2.03378202e-31  3.52522217e-30  5.96576060e-30
    1.00000000e-06  1.73549399e-29  2.38630424e-29  4.06756404e-30
    1.62702562e-29]
  [-2.39813715e-28  2.36658272e-30  4.10207671e-29  6.94197597e-29
    1.73549399e-29  1.00000000e-06  2.77679039e-28  4.73316543e-29
    1.89326617e-28]
  [-3.29743858e-28  3.25405123e-30  5.64035547e-29  9.54521695e-29
    2.38630424e-29  2.77679039e-28  1.00000000e-06  6.50810247e-29
    2.60324099e-28]


  [-5.62063395e-29  5.54667824e-31  9.61424228e-30  1.62702562e-29
    4.06756404e-30  4.73316543e-29  6.50810247e-29  1.00000000e-06
    4.43734259e-29]
  [-2.24825358e-28  2.21867130e-30  3.84569691e-29  6.50810247e-29
    1.62702562e-29  1.89326617e-28  2.60324099e-28  4.43734259e-29
    1.00000000e-06]]

    #long output was omitted
]
convergent =  True
```

The information about specific clusters can be obtained by the following code:

```
labels = gm.fit_predict(scores)
print("Labels = ", labels)
print("etiquettes = ", df_scores.index)
print("clusters = ", list(zip(labels, df_scores.index)))
```

that gives:

```
Labels =  [6 6 4 4 6 5 6 2 3 3 7 4 0 3 4 6 1 2 2 2]
etiquettes =  Index(['Q5.1' , 'Q5.2' , 'Q5.3' , 'Q5.4' , 'Q5.5' , 'Q5.6',
            'Q5.7' , 'Q5.8' , 'Q5.9' , 'Q5.10' , 'Q5.11' , 'Q5.12',
            'Q5,13' , 'Q5.14' , 'Q5.15' , 'Q5.16' , 'Q5.17' , 'Q5.18',
            'Q5.19' , 'Q5.20'],
      dtype='object')
clusters =  [(6, 'Q5.1'), (6, 'Q5.2'), (4, 'Q5.3'), (4, 'Q5.4'),
            (6, 'Q5.5'), (5, 'Q5.6'), (6, 'Q5.7'), (2, 'Q5.8'),
            (3, 'Q5.9'), (3, 'Q5.10'), (7, 'Q5.11'), (4, 'Q5.12'),
            (0, 'Q5.13'), (3, 'Q5.14'), (4, 'Q5.15'), (6, 'Q5.16'),
            (1, 'Q5.17'), (2, 'Q5.18'), (2, 'Q5.19'), (2, 'Q5.20')]
```

The content of clusters is summarised in Table 6.3. These clusters can be compared with k-means output. Both of these approaches can provide different clusters that can give complementary insight into the phenomena under consideration.

In Table 6.3, the cluster three collects the opinion about the boss. The cluster four connects a clear description of the work responsibilities with initiative, fulfilling demands at work, and good relations with colleagues.

Table 6.3 GMM clusters for *Q5*.

Cluster number	Members
0	Q5.13
1	Q5.17
2	Q5.8, Q5.18, Q5.19, Q5.20
3	Q5.9, Q5.10, Q5.14
4	Q5.3, Q5.4, Q5.12, Q5.15
5	Q5.6
6	Q5.1, Q5.2, Q5.5, Q5.7, Q5.16
7	Q5.11

The plot projected on the space spanned by the first three PCs is realised by:

```
from matplotlib import pyplot
from mpl_toolkits.mplot3d import Axes3D
from numpy.random import rand
from pylab import figure

fig = figure()

fig = plt.figure(figsize=plt.figaspect(0.5)*1.5)
ax = fig.gca(projection='3d')
ax = Axes3D(fig)

ax.scatter(scores[:,0],scores[:,1],scores[:,2], c=labels, s=200, cmap='viridis')

for i in range(len(scores[:,0])):
    ax.text(scores[i,0],scores[i,1],scores[i,2],  '%s' % (df_scores.index[i]), \
    size=15, zorder=1,  color='k')

centers = gm.means_
ax.scatter(centers[:, 0], centers[:, 1], centers[:, 2], c='red' , marker='+' , \
s=300, alpha=0.5, label="Cluster means");
ax.legend(loc="lower left")

plt.grid(True)
ax.set_xlabel("PC1 ({:.1f}%)".format(pca_out.explained_variance_ratio_[0]*100))
ax.set_ylabel("PC2 ({:.1f}%)".format(pca_out.explained_variance_ratio_[1]*100))
ax.set_zlabel("PC3 ({:.1f}%)".format(pca_out.explained_variance_ratio_[2]*100))

plt.savefig("GaussianPCA9-3dim.png")
```

where the centers of the Gaussians are collected in centers= gm.means_ . The plot is saved in the file GaussianPCA9–3dim.png and presented in Figure 6.13.

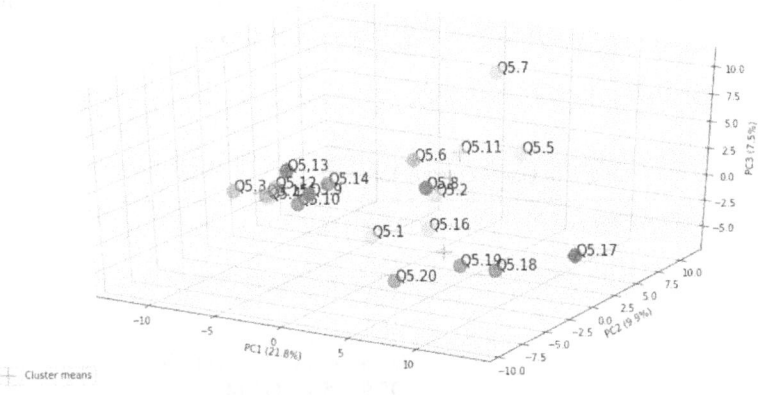

Figure 6.13 GMM clusters for *Q5*.

6.2 Summary

In this chapter, a hands-on approach to the analysis of answers to the questionnaire related to Generation Z employees' engagement at the workplace, using Python and Scikit-learn library, was presented. These techniques help to extract information on the association between various (answers to) questions in the questionnaire. With a bit of engagement, the provided code can be adapted to a different research situation.

By no means does this chapter exhaust the possibilities of application of machine learning methods to management research. However, it is hoped that the presented results will encourage the reader to experiment with the example and adjust it to specific needs. For more advanced approaches, one should consult [5, 1, 4].

Notes

1 More detailed distinction is presented in, e.g., [1].
2 See: https://scikit-learn.org/stable/auto_examples/mixture/plot_gmm_selection. html#sphx-glr-auto-examples-mixture-plot-gmm-selection-py.

Bibliography

[1] Gèron A. (2019), *Hands-On Machine Learning with Scikit-Learn, Keras, and TensorFlow: Concepts, Tools, and Techniques to Build Intelligent Systems*, 2nd edition, O'Reilly Media.

[2] Jolliffe I.T. (2002), *Principal Component Analysis*, 2nd edition, Springer New York, NY.

[3] Kycia R.A., Niemczynowicz A., Niezurawska-Zajac J. (2021), Towards the global vision of engagement of generation Z at the workplace: Mathematical modeling, Proceedings of 37th International Business Information Management Association Conference (IBIMA), pp. 6084–6095 (2021); ISBN: 978-0-9998551-6-4.

[4] Müller A.C., Guido S. (2016), *Introduction to Machine Learning with Python: A Guide for Data Scientists*, 1st edition, O'Reilly Media.

[5] Raschka S., Mirjalili V. (2017), *Python Machine Learning: Second Edition: Machine Learning and Deep Learning with Python, Scikit-Learn, and TensorFlow*, 2nd edition, Packt Publishing.

[6] Scikit-Learn Library Documentation. https://scikit-learn.org (accessed: 11.06.2021).

[7] GitHub. https://github.com/rkycia/GenerationZBookCode (accessed: 21.09.2022).

7 Recommendation for entrepreneurs

Nelson Duarte and Carla Pereira

7.1 How should employers treat Generation Z employees?

This is one of the questions found in this book, and somehow, we will try to answer it in this chapter. After reading the different chapters of this book, it is clear that a simple answer does not exist. Anyway, in this chapter, we will summarise the conclusions from different researches to provide some practical guidelines to employers.

Another important issue that was discussed in this book is the work-related demands, needs, and values for Generation Z in comparison to other generations. On one hand, some employers and organisations express concerns about the way to manage the existence of four generations (at the same time) in current organisations. On the other hand, organisations are aware that talent acquisition and retention might be more important nowadays than it was some years ago. Currently, there is a growing number of employers and human resources (HR) professionals involved in the demystification of the career models for younger generations. The extent to which an individual finds a well-fitting job represents the individual's overall positive judgement of his or her future life and career. Some researchers even argue that is possible to find a positive correlation between job and life satisfaction.

Bearing in mind that the model of a job for a lifetime is also an old-fashioned concept and younger generations are willing to have different experiences and realising that change is part of their life. To move from one to another company, from one to another job, is not a problem for this generation. However, this willingness to change, crucial for survival, might be a problem for employers, in particular for those that are trying to retain talent in their organisations. These changes generate an increase in costs, weaker results, and higher staff fluctuation.

The important mindset for change that seems to be more present in younger generations presents itself as a positive aspect for employers in terms of talent acquisition and market demands but might be a real problem

DOI: 10.4324/9781003353935-7

when it comes to talent retention. To promote talent retention, employers are looking for new solutions in the area of HR management. The introduction of a new motivation approach is becoming imperative to increase the level of engagement and loyalty among employees. *So how can companies keep talent?*

To try to answer the last question, and to characterise Generation Z (those born after 1994), a group of researchers from the Czech Republic, Latvia, Poland, and Portugal have been working on this topic. The main goal of this project was to find generational diversity at the workplace and to identify effective tools for motivating and rewarding employees of Generation Z.

Another important factor that was considered while developing the project and the researches associated was the hygge concept. Hygge comes from Scandinavia, and it has gained popularity in Europe, America, and Asia. Hygge for the Danes means cosiness, comfort, and joy [2]. Even being a concept that was born to describe a lifestyle, hygge works well in a commercial setting [3]. In the latter, hygge can be applied in most of the HR management areas, but also in the way the organisation operates in the business environment. The main areas where hygge can be implemented include: motivating the employees, work organisations, but also on issues related to the structures within the organisations or business activities [4].

According to [6], hygge in the commercial setting is characterized by the presence of greenery whose aim is to relax and calm down the employees during their work. Another need connected with work is equalisation and transparency at the workplace, which translates to equality of all employees and transparency of motivating and remuneration policies. Fair play and lack of aggressive behaviours is yet another need accounted for in the pyramid of employees' needs carried out according to the concept of hygge.

After this, another question arises: *How important is this hygge approach for today's companies?* Or, from another perspective, *how seriously do the younger generations take this concept for their career decisions?*

To better understand the concept of hygge in companies, it is important to clarify by now what was being analysed during the conducted research. For the questionnaires that were applied, the concept of hygge in companies was divided as follows:

- Work-life balance: Keeping the balance between private and professional life.
- Workplace: Cosy, interestingly designed office space, and the presence of greenery with eco-friendly elements.
- Organisational structure: Flat organisational structure, egalitarianism, and transparency at the workplace.

- Activities in business (social responsibility): Fair play and lack of aggressive business actions on the market.
- Organisational culture: Culture includes mutual respect, a culture of teamwork, integration and communication, as well as the key role of the manager or leader.
- Motivating employees: Engagement of employees based on good relations, clarity of goals and rules, proper work evaluation, and feedback from the employer/manager.

Presented are the main aspects that were analysed during this project. We will present some of the most relevant results obtained. The results are related to specifically studied samples, and those samples are identified before the presentation of the results. We will also add some discussion about the results obtained.

Main results:

- From a survey of 18,000 professionals and students across Generations X, Y, and Z from 19 countries conducted by INSEAD, it was found that Generation Z individuals favoured working for an international company, while Generations Y and X professionals preferred starting their own business. However, these intentions differ among countries.
- A survey of 1,195 individuals from four different generations (Baby Boomers, X, Y, and Z) from Latvia, Poland, and Portugal analysed seven different factors related to job motivation: (1) excitement and global focus, (2) comfort, (3) achievement, (4) supervision; (5) technologies, (6) independence, (7) altruism. Results show that the work-related factors of the four studied generations are not so different: *independence is more important for older generations, while excitement and technologies are more important for younger generations.* These results from European research are aligned with those found in a study from 2010 in China [7]. Moreover, [1] also concluded that *Generation Z was most enthusiastic about technologies as well as the potential of virtual reality.*
- From the same research, it was possible to verify *that when comparing material, non-material, and hygge motivators, hygge* (or well-being factors) *are presented as the most important ones, followed by material factors.* When comparing different generation results, *it was found that Generation Z put more value on material and non-material motivators than other generations.*
- On what regards material motivators, *the most relevant for Generation Z are educational bonuses, healthy lifestyle benefits, childcare benefits, insurances, and retirement benefits* (this one was considered more

important for Baby Boomers). However, it is important to mention that most of the *Generation Z individuals that participated in this research are not yet working*. This lack of experience at work-life may influence the answers presented by the individuals of this generation.

- Considering non-material motivators, *Generation Z stands on work security*. This generation aims to have a permanent work contract. They will prefer to work in a public sector organisation. They would highly value working in a socially responsible company—one which engages in local matters, social and ecological issues, and which aids local entrepreneurship. They also, more than other generations, put importance on working in a dynamically developing business—a company with a high-profit rate, high profitability, and constantly increasing its market share.

- Generation Y individuals (those born from 1980 to 1995) appear to differ from other generations, giving more importance to factors such as work-life balance, the organisational culture, and the motivation from the leaders.

- *Generation Z* seems to be a generation that prefers to have options. For this generation, *the important well-being factor is the possibility of choosing benefits from a list offered by the employer*.

- A research study done in Poland included the opinion of 900 individuals and found that *employees' engagement is directly related to the non-material instruments of motivation*, namely, work security, social responsibility from the company's side, flexible working hours, remote work, the relationships among teams, and being part of a dynamically developing business. *These non-material motivators are also known as emotional salaries*.

- *Another important factor to promote employees' engagement was found to be the hygge concept* adoption, and *only in third place comes the financial motivation*. Anyway, it is important not to forget about Maslow's hierarchy of needs: the lower-level needs such as salary must first be met. Then companies should target the higher-level needs to get the engagement from their employees.

- By working on engagement conditions from their employees, companies are also promoting their loyalty, since the latter research found out that *engagement presents a positive impact on loyalty*. Even finding some results that might seem contradictory, such as a negative impact from non-material instruments and hygge in loyalty, this negative impact seems to be not significant. Even not existing as a direct positive impact, it exists indirectly through employees' engagement. Quite interesting to notice is that when comparing results among different generations, *the impact of engagement on loyalty is significantly different from Baby Boomers to Generation Z, being stronger for the latter*.

- One other research conducted in Poland in 2018 focusing on individuals from Generation Z (200 participants), it was concluded that employee satisfaction presents a relation with challenging and interesting work. Efficient work by employees is promoted by the existence of a good work environment among colleagues. *Clarification of employees' responsibilities is a key to work-life balance.* This might mean that individuals from this generation want to know what they are responsible for. In this way, apparently, they will easily manage their professional and private life.

- Another activity from this research group was a quantitative study conducted in Poland, Latvia, and Portugal with a total number of participants of 2,269 belonging to four different generations (Baby Boomers, Generations X, Y, and Z). *One of the conclusions allowed to identify those workplace aspects which can be characterised as hygge as the most important workplace motivators.* For some reason that was not yet identified, hygge is especially important for Portuguese respondents.

- From the study referred to in the last bullet, it was possible to conclude that on overall analysis, *hygge is assumed as the most relevant factor, followed by the material motivators, and then the non-material ones.* These results are not aligned with those from the 900 individuals studied in the Polish research, where financial motivators got the third position. In fact, in the study from 2018 in Poland, financial motivators were identified as the most relevant ones. Once the research was conducted with different individuals, it take us back to Maslow's hierarchy of needs. It is known that individuals will only care about the upper level after having the previous level needs satisfied. The different results obtained in both pieces of research might indicate that the respondents (in this case from Poland) were in different levels of Maslow's pyramid.

- Also interesting to notice that gender must be taken into consideration. According to the results, *hygge motivators are more important for females* than for males. At the same time, *hygge and non-material motivators are more important for respondents with higher levels of education.* Assuming that higher levels of education lead to better job positions and salaries, it can be assumed that once satisfied of their the basic needs, individuals are looking for other types of rewards in their organisational life.

- Considering the hygge factors listed above, this research also analysed the most important ones. They all scored above 3.5 on a 0 to 5 scale, but *factors that promote balance between private and professional life and the organisationsal culture stand from all the others.* On the other hand, the workplace factor (cosy and interestingly designed office space), scored the lowest value.

Summing up the most relevant conclusions, one can say that as found by [5], millennials, and we can add younger generations, have grown up during the Information Age, they connected to each other and use technology for work, for fun or when information is needed, thus they value technologies. On what regards different types of motivations, the results are not clear. Some present financial motivators as the most relevant ones, some others (the non-financial) as the most important for younger generations. We believe that all of them are important. An employee that does not earn enough to satisfy his/hers basic needs will hardly be engaged with the organisations. But once the financial needs are satisfied, organisations must care about the non-material motivators in order to retain their resources. Relevance to balance between private and professional life, and organisational culture are elements that managers and HR responsible must pay attention to nowadays.

Bibliography

[1] Bresman H., Rao V.D. (2017), *A survey of 19 countries shows how generations X, Y, and Z are—and aren't—different*, Harvard Business Review, 25 August. https://hbr.org/2017/08/a-survey-of-19-countries-shows-how-generations-x-y-and-z-are-and-arent-different (accessed: 15.11.2021).

[2] Linnet J.T. (2011), *Money can't buy me hygge: Danish middle-class consumption, egalitarianism, and the sanctity of inner space*, Social Analysis, 22–24.

[3] Linnet J.T. (2012), *The social-material performance of cozy interiority*, In Ambiances in Action/Ambiances en acte (s)-International Congress on Ambiances, International Ambiances Network, 403.

[4] Lugosi P. (2009), *The production of hospitable space: Commercial propositions and consumer co-creation in a bar operation*, Space and Culture, 12(4), 396–411.

[5] Mitkova L., Mariak V. (2015), *The first globalized generation—generation Y*, 15th International Scientific Conference Globalization and Its Socio-Economic Consequences, University of Zilina, Zilina.

[6] Nieżurawska-Zajac J. (2020), *Motywowanie w zarzadzaniu różnorodnościa pokoleniowa* (Motivating in Managing of Generational Diversity), Poland: CDEWU, p. 420.

[7] Yi X., Ribbens B., Morgan C.N. (2010), *Generational differences in China: Career implications*, Career Development International, 15(6), 601–620.

8   Conclusions

*Joanna Nieżurawska, Radosław Antoni Kycia,
and Agnieszka Niemczynowicz*

The new approach to motivation brings about many changes, including changes in social processes (new behaviour patterns) and demographic changes (ageing of societies). The new generation that is entering professional life, born in the age of the Internet and smartphones, remains diametrically different from the generation of their parents or grandparents. For the latter, work that gives a sense of happiness is an incomprehensible construct, and maintaining the balance between work and life is a whim. The norm for them is commitment and loyalty. In an organisation that is faced with the need to use the vigour and freshness of youth as well as the experience and wisdom of older people, intergenerational cooperation is important. This potential must be used as best as possible, and this is an extremely difficult task. All the more so as the development generated inequalities that unleashed a wave of populism which, in turn, created new divisions.

Loyalty and commitment are the paradigm of modern management science. They are the basis for motivating set in the realities of the 21st century. However, is it achievable in the face of contemporary phenomena? We can only try to answer the question of what to do and how to do it to create a motivational instrumentation taking into account the diversity factor, which will trigger high loyalty and commitment in employees. Modern concepts of motivating, therefore, take into account the diversification of employee groups in terms of age by proposing motivating instruments that are aimed at satisfying their different needs and aspirations. Undoubtedly, this is a condition for improving the effectiveness of the incentive systems of modern enterprises.

From among the many criteria for the differentiation of labour resources generating a different approach to motivating, generation diversity was selected for analysis. It is not an accidental procedure. Although there appeared a lot of literature concerning the issue of generational diversity, it clearly lacks comprehensive studies on the different priorities towards life

DOI: 10.4324/9781003353935-8

and work, expectations and aspirations, attitudes and behaviours examining Generations BB, X, Y, and Z active on the market at the same time.

Analyses of implementation effectiveness of the motivation concept contain a clear gap in diagnosing their impact on building engagement and loyalty of employees of each generation. The gap results from the lack of diagnosis of the youngest generation, Z, and their preferences in terms of motivation. This work is an attempt to fill this gap.

The results of the research presented in this book confirm the correctness of the topic selection, and the results of the research in the cross-section of selected countries are very interesting. The adopted method of analysis may contribute to further research on motivating in diversity management, including generational diversity. The attempt made in the book to assess the usefulness of selected motivation concepts in building engagement and loyalty of employees from various generations, as well as an attempt to formulate a general model showing the relationship between employee commitment and loyalty and on other hand the instruments and concepts of motivating, can be valuable both from a scientific and practical point of view.

Moreover, exploring the problem of motivation carries a utilitarian value. Finding the key to human motivation, including work motivation, is a milestone for effective motivating. All managers and employers know about it. Although the largest companies in the world compete in offering new payroll, non-financial, and non-material solutions, there is still a noticeable decline in engagement and loyalty among employees. Motivating people to work is one of the most difficult management functions. Activating the human resources' potential requires not only economic knowledge but also an understanding of the psychological nature of man. Therefore, a question arises whether a human in an organisation is its strategic resource since the human factor is unreliable and unpredictable.

The current times of the pandemic are a time of trials and changes, especially on the labour market. They will certainly set new directions for research on motivation that will influence the increase in engagement and loyalty of the young generation, i.e. Gen Z.

Limitation

While the authors hope that the study provides some guidance on how to predict the motivation of Generation Z based on traditional motivation systems, they are aware that it is not without limitations. The first limitation is because the authors focus on relations taking place at one level of analysis, i.e., at the organisational level. Yet another limitation is looking at employees from a generational perspective. One should be aware that generation is an important, though not the only, factor ensuring the loyalty level. Generations are influenced by extraordinary events that may be radically different across the world. Similar is the case in terms of trends that may take place at different times in individual countries. On the other hand, we are aware that the research carried out has a limited territorial scope. The authors plan to conduct further studies with an extended territorial scope soon.

Appendix A

Research questionnaire A

This is the motivating and rewarding employees in relation to their engagement and loyalty at work as seen by Generations/Armstrong Engagement Questionnaire, see [1].

Motivating and rewarding employees in relation to their engagement and loyalty at work as seen by Generations X, Y, Z

S1. Which of the following aspects of motivation and remuneration systems are important to you?

- 5. Very important
- 4. Important
- 3. Moderately important
- 2. Not so important
- 1. Unimportant

1. Level of total reward gross (including all the benefits)
2. Level of additional premiums (functional allowance, service, and shift premiums)
3. Appreciation bonuses (dependent on the manager's appreciation)
4. Educational bonuses (subsidies for education)
5. Health benefits: Medicover, Luxmed cards, access to doctors and specialists
6. Healthy lifestyle benefits (MultiSport cards, access to swimming pools, gyms)
7. Childcare benefits (subsidies for nurseries, kindergarten, summer camps)
8. Additional benefits (insurance benefits: life insurance, accident insurance, group insurance)
9. Retirement and pension benefits systems

10. Work security (permanent employment contract, managerial contract, tenure, etc.)
11. Working in public service company or a state-owned company
12. Working in a socially responsible company (one which engages in local matters, social and ecological issues, and which aids local entrepreneurship)
13. Working in a multinational enterprise (opportunities to work in multinational projects, business trips)
14. Flexible working hours
15. Remote work (at least one day a week)
16. Good atmosphere at work (good relations with the boss and co-workers)
17. Working in a dynamically developing business (company with high profit rate, high profitability, increasing its market share)

S2. Are you satisfied with the company you work for with regards to the following aspects of motivation and remuneration systems of employees?

- 5. Fully satisfied
- 4. Satisfied to a great extent
- 3. Satisfied with some, not satisfied with others
- 2. Satisfied to a little extent
- 1. Not satisfied at all

1. Level of total reward gross (including all the benefits)
2. Level of additional premiums (functional allowance, service, and shift premiums)
3. Bonus systems depend on individual results
4. Appreciation bonuses (dependent on the manager's appreciation)
5. Educational bonuses (subsidising education)
6. Health benefits: Medicover, Luxmed cards, access to doctors and specialists
7. Healthy lifestyle benefits (MultiSport cards, access to swimming pools, gyms)
8. Childcare benefits (subsidies to nurseries, preschools, summer camps)
9. Additional benefits (insurance benefits: life insurance, accident insurance, group insurance)
10. Retirement and pension benefits systems

11. Work security (permanent employment contract, managerial contract, tenure, etc.)
12. Working in public service company or a state-owned company
13. Working in a socially responsible corporate (one which engages in local matters, social and ecological issues, and which aids local entrepreneurship)
14. Working in a multinational enterprise (opportunities to work in multinational projects, business trips)
15. Flexible working hours
16. Remote work (at least one day a week)
17. Good work atmosphere (good relations with the boss and co-workers)
18. Working in a dynamically developing business (company with high profit rate, high profitability, increasing its market share)

S3. How important are the following modern systems and concepts of remuneration and motivation for you?

- 5. Very important
- 4. Important
- 3. Moderately important
- 2. Not so important
- 1. Unimportant

1. Work-life balance concept (keeping balance between your private and professional life)
2. Cafeteria system (possibility of choosing your own benefits from a list offered by the employer)
3. Flexible remuneration system (wages are adjusted to the employee's competencies and results)
4. Concept of "hygge" which emphasises cosy and interestingly designed office space with plants and eco-friendly elements
5. Concept of "hygge" with a flat organisational structure, egalitarianism, and transparency at the workplace
6. Concept of "hygge" which emphasises fair play and includes not taking aggressive actions on the business market
7. Concept of "hygge" which emphasises organisational culture which includes respect towards one another, teamwork, integration, and communication
8. Concept of "hygge" which emphasises the role of the manager—leader—who positively motivates the employees, is available to everyone, and is part of the team.

S4. Are you satisfied with the company you work for with regards to the following aspects of modern systems and concepts of remuneration and motivation?

- 5. Fully satisfied
- 4. Satisfied to a great extent
- 3. Satisfied with some, not satisfied with others
- 2. Satisfied to a little extent
- 1. Not satisfied at all

    1. Work-life balance concept (keeping balance between your private and professional life)
    2. Cafeteria system (possibility of choosing your own benefits from a list offered by the employer)
    3. Flexible remuneration system (wages are adjusted to the employee's competencies and results)
    4. Concept of "hygge" which emphasises cosy and interestingly designed office space with plants and eco-friendly elements
    5. Concept of "hygge" with a flat organisational structure, egalitarianism, and transparency at the workplace
    6. Concept of "hygge" which emphasises fair play and includes not taking aggressive actions at the business market
    7. Concept of "hygge" which emphasises organisational culture which includes respect towards each other, teamwork, integration, and communication
    8. Concept of "hygge" which emphasises the role of the manager—leader—who positively motivates the employees, is available to everyone, and is part of the team.

S5. Do you agree with the statements below about your engagement at your workplace?

- 5. I fully agree
- 4. I agree
- 3. I'm not sure
- 2. I don't agree
- 1. I fully disagree

    1. I'm very satisfied with the work I do
    2. My job is interesting
    3. I know exactly what I'm expected to do
    4. I am prepared to show initiative to do my work well
    5. My job is challenging (sets new goals, is prospective)
    6. I have plenty of freedom on how to do my work

7. I get plenty of opportunities to learn in this job
8. The facilities/equipment/tools provided are excellent
9. I have a lot of support from my boss
10. My boss recognises my work
11. The experience I am getting now will be of great help in advancing my future career
12. I find it easy to keep up with the demands of my job
13. I have no problems in achieving balance between my professional and private life
14. I like working with my boss
15. I get on well with my work colleagues
16. I think this organisation is a great place to work
17. I believe I have a great future in this organisation
18. I intend to go on working for this organisation
19. I am happy about the values of this organisation—how it conducts its business
20. The products/services provided by this organisation are excellent

S6. Do you agree with the statement below about your loyalty to the employer?

- 5. I fully agree
- 4. I agree
- 3. I'm not sure
- 2. I don't agree
- 1. I fully disagree

1. I defend the good name of this company
2. I feel proud of my work
3. I strongly feel that I'm part of this company
4. I keep professional secrets
5. My company matters greatly to me
6. My company is an authority for me
7. I'm a loyal employee
8. I intend to go on working for this organisation

Respondent's particulars

Gender

- male
- female

Education

- elementary
- high school (matura exam[1] or equivalent)
- higher education
- higher education plus postgraduate studies (or doctoral studies)

Employment

- Yes—I'm employed (full-time job, managerial contract, internship)
- Yes—I'm employed (mandatory agreement, contract of commission)
- No—I'm unemployed, but I'm studying (student)
- No—I'm unemployed (I'm neither studying nor working)

Position in the company

- senior manager (managers)
- lower-level manager and specialists
- administrative employees—office
- other employees

Years in this organisation

- less than one year
- one to five years
- six to ten years
- over 11 years

Industry you're working in

- education
- administration
- insurance
- construction
- medical
- food
- IT
- automotive
- other industry (please write your industry in the field below)

Size of your company/institution

- micro
- small

- medium
- large

Does your company operate on the global market?

- Yes
- No

Is your company a multi-ethnic company (hires people from different countries)?

- Yes
- No

Age (born between)

- 1995–2004 (Generation Z)
- 1980–1994 (Generation Y)
- 1965–1979 (Generation X)
- 1946–1964 (Baby Boomers)
- 1925–1945 (Traditionalists)

NATIONALITY

Country of residence

Note

1 * Matura exam is an exam that students take at the end of secondary school. Passing it enables a student to apply for university and continue their education.

Bibliography

[1]   Armstrong M. (2009), *Armstrong's Handbook of Performance Management: An Evidence-Based Guide to Delivering High Performance*, Kogan Page Publishers London, United Kingdom, 332.

Appendix B

Research questionnaire B

This is the work importance/motivation questionnaire used in Chapter 4. Minnesota Importance Questionnaire [1] is updated by adding new items related to the contemporary workplace.

Work importance/motivation questionnaire

S1. Please think about your ideal job and name three most important associations which come to your mind (these may be related to the job content, organisation, yourself, or similar).

1.
2.
3.

S2. Please think about your ideal job and indicate how important these factors are for you.

- 5. Very important
- 4. Important
- 3. Moderately important
- 2. Not so important
- 1. Unimportant

On my ideal job, it is important that:

1. I make use of my abilities
2. the work could give me a feeling of accomplishment
3. I could be busy all the time
4. the job would provide an opportunity for advancement
5. I could give directions and instructions to others
6. I would be treated fairly by the company
7. my pay would compare well with that of other workers

8. my co-workers would be easy to get along with
9. I could try out my own ideas
10. I could work alone
11. I would never be pressured to do things that go against my sense of right and wrong
12. I could receive recognition for the work I do
13. I could make decisions on my own
14. the job would provide for steady employment
15. I could do things for other people
16. I would be looked up to by others in my company and my community
17. I have supervisors who would back up their workers with management
18. I would have supervisors who train workers well
19. I could do something different every day
20. the job would have good working conditions
21. I could plan my work with little supervision
22. I could do something exciting every day
23. I could work with new technologies
24. I could use modern IT (e.g., cloud computing; video conferencing)
25. I could work with artificial intelligence
26. the job would have a global focus
27. I could work with colleagues from different cultures
28. I can start my own business

S3: Please indicate how important the following aspects of motivation systems are for you.

- 5. Very important
- 4. Important
- 3. Moderately important
- 2. Not so important
- 1. Unimportant

   1. Level of total reward gross (including all the benefits)
   2. Level of additional premiums (functional allowance, service, and shift premiums)
   3. Bonus systems depend on individual results
   4. Appreciation bonuses (dependent on the manager's appreciation)
   5. Educational bonuses (subsidies for education)

6. Health benefits: Medicover, Luxmed cards, access to doctors and specialists
7. Healthy lifestyle benefits (MultiSport cards, access to swimming pools, gyms)
8. Childcare benefits (subsidies for nurseries, kindergarten, summer camps)
9. Additional benefits (insurance benefits: life insurance, accident insurance, group insurance)
10. Retirement and pension benefits systems
11. Work security (permanent employment contract, managerial contract, tenure, etc.)
12. Working in public service company or a state-owned company
13. Working in a socially responsible company (one which engages in local matters, social and ecological issues, and which aids local entrepreneurship)
14. Working in a multinational enterprise (opportunities to work in a multinational project, business trips)
15. Flexible working hours
16. Remote work (work from home at least one day a week)
17. Working in a dynamically developing business (company with high profit rate, high profitability, increasing its market share)

S4. How important are the following concepts of motivation for you?

- 5. Very important
- 4. Important
- 3. Moderately important
- 2. Not so important
- 1. Unimportant

1. keeping balance between your private and professional life
2. possibility of choosing my own benefits from a list offered by the employer
3. wages are adjusted to the employee's competencies and results
4. cosy and interestingly designed office space with plants and eco-friendly elements
5. flat organisational structure, egalitarianism, and transparency at the workplace
6. employer is socially responsible (including "fair play" and not taking aggressive actions on the business market)
7. organisational culture which includes respect towards one another, teamwork, integration, and communication
8. the manager/ leader positively motivates the employees, is available to everyone, and is part of the team

Respondent's particulars

Gender

- male
- female
- other

Education

- elementary
- high school (matura exam[1] or equivalent)
- higher education
- higher education plus postgraduate studies (or doctoral studies)

Employment

- Yes—I'm employed (full-time job, managerial contract, internship)
- Yes—I'm employed (mandatory agreement, contract of commission)
- No—I'm unemployed, but I'm studying (student)
- No—I'm unemployed (I'm neither studying nor working)

Age (born between)

- 1995–2004 (Generation Z)
- 1980–1994 (Generation Y)
- 1965–1979 (Generation X)
- 1946–1964 (Baby Boomers)
- 1925–1945 (Traditionalists)

NATIONALITY

Note

1 Matura exam is an exam that students take at the end of secondary school. Passing it enables a student to apply for university and continue their education.

Bibliography

[1]   Weiss D.J., Dawis R.V., England G.W., Lofquist L.H. (1964), *Construct Validation Studies of the Minnesota Importance Questionnaire*, Minnesota: Studies in Vocational Rehabilitation.

Index